Southern Rolling Stock in Colour

Mike King

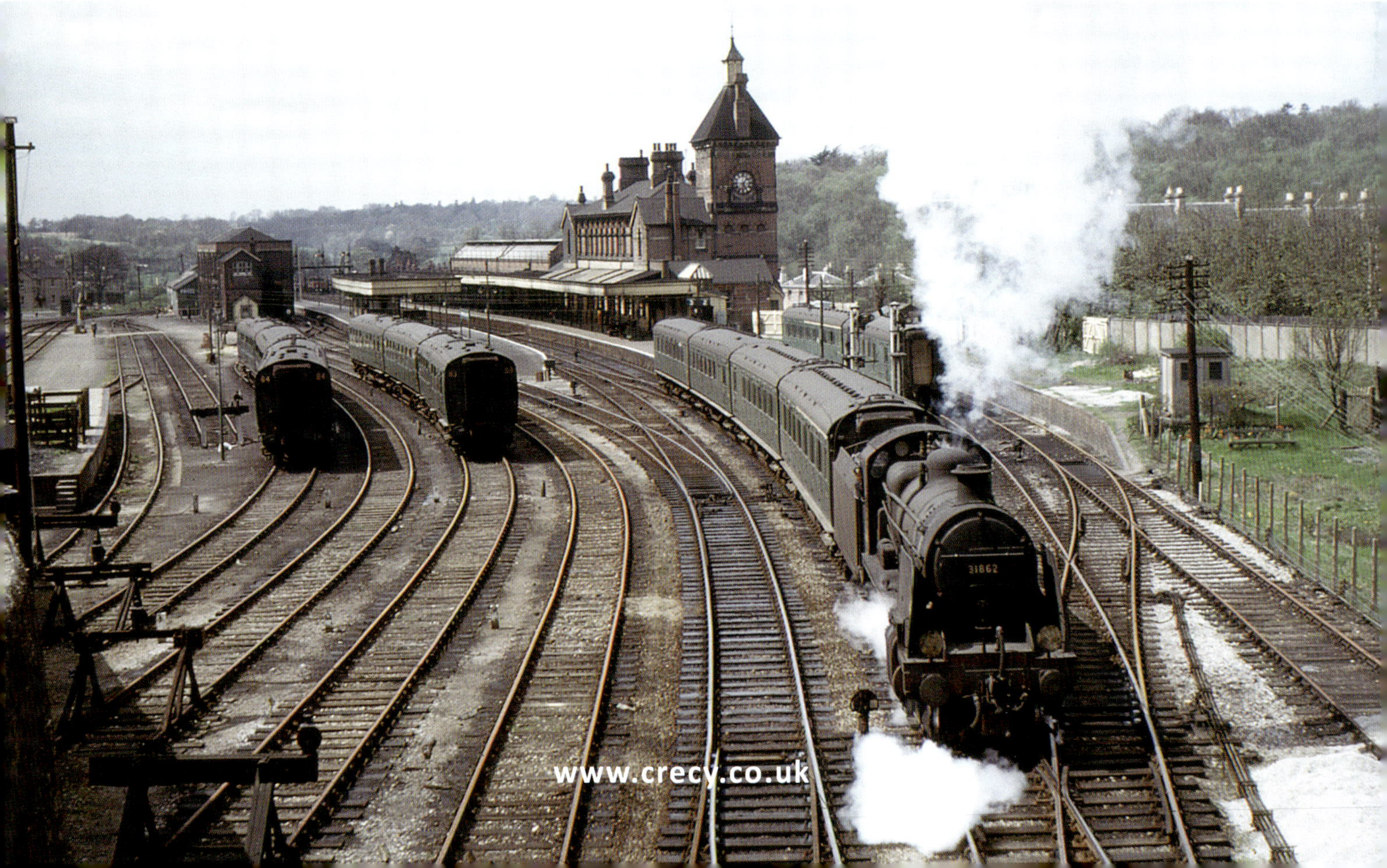

www.crecy.co.uk

© 2015 Mike King

ISBN 978-1-909328-41-9

First published in 2016 by Crécy Publishing Ltd

All editorial submissions to:
The Southern Way (Kevin Robertson)
PO Box 279
Corhampton
Southampton SO32 3ZX
Tel: 01489 877880
editorial@thesouthernway.co.uk

All rights reserved. No part of this book may be reproduced or transmitted in any form or by any means electronic or mechanical, including photocopying, recording or by any information storage without permission from the Publisher in writing. All enquiries should be directed to the Publisher.

A CIP record for this book is available from the British Library

Publisher's note: Every effort has been made to identify and correctly attribute photographic credits. Any error that may have occurred is entirely unintentional.

Printed in Slovenia by GPS Print

Crécy Publishing Limited
1a Ringway Trading Estate
Shadowmoss Road
Manchester M22 5LH

www.crecy.co.uk

Front Cover, main view: SR milk tank No 4408 at Swindon Works in 1980. This was built in November 1931 as a four-wheeler, being reframed in either April 1937 or April 1938 – the records are slightly garbled – and by the 1970s was being operated by Unigate Creameries. To the Southern Railway, this was a "milk tank type 1 converted". An article in The Southern Railway Magazine for March 1933 described the vehicles, noting that the Southern had by then 25 tanks (or trucks for road tankers) in use for the bulk transportation of milk – the tanks carried 3,000 gallons and the product was kept fresh by the interior of the tank being insulated and glass-lined. At that time they were mostly to be found as 'tail' traffic on passenger trains but it was expected that as the type was multiplied, whole trains of them would be run. By the 1960s, never mind 1980, any semblance of colourful livery had gone and a dull, uninspiring dirty silver/grey colour prevailed, with just a small metal plate indicating ownership and numbering. Milk traffic, as far as the Southern Region was concerned, had largely ceased in the late 1960s and the vehicles saw out their time on Western Region services from Cornwall, Devon and Wales to London, even if their ultimate city destination still took them over SR metals. By 1980 milk traffic by rail had practically ceased but there were hopes of a revival so a number of wagons were retained in store at Swindon Works. This was not to be and for tank No 4408 breaking up finally took place in late 1980 or 1981. *M Rhodes*

Front cover, bottom left: Breakdown packing van No ADS4 at Stewarts Lane in July 1985. An even-planked van, this was built in June 1935 as SR No 1189, to Diagram 3103 and entered departmental service in November 1953.
R C Riley, courtesy Rodney Lissenden

Front cover, centre bottom: Pullman camping coach No SC41 at Morar, on the line to Mallaig, finished in pale blue livery on 2nd July 1962. This was formerly parlour first Sunbeam. *M Rhodes*

Front cover, bottom right: BR-built special cattle van No S3736S actually on the move in a van train at Reading in 1967 – by then a rare sight. *M Rhodes*

Rear: What became the standard British Railways corridor coach livery from April 1949 until June 1956 – crimson lake and cream – is seen on the 11.54am Waterloo-Salisbury train passing Weybridge behind Bulleid pacific No 34054 Lord Beaverbrook early in 1957. The stock comprises Bulleid three-set type L No 770, augmented to five vehicles by the addition of two unspecified Diagram 2019 corridor thirds – these being the second and fourth vehicles and identifiable by their 15in deep window vents. The other three coaches are Diagram 2123 semi-open brake thirds Nos 4301/2 and prototype Diagram 2315 Bulleid composite No 5751 in the centre. Three 'utility' vans bring up the rear of the train. *F Foote*

Contents

Introduction 4

Section One –
Pre-Grouping Passenger Stock 5

Section Two –
Post-Grouping Passenger Stock 41

Section Three –
Pullman Cars 60

Section Four –
Utility Vans and Other Non-Passenger
Coaching Stock 69

Section Five –
Milk Tank Wagons 80

Section Six –
Pre-Grouping Wagons 88

Section Seven –
Post-Grouping Wagons 103

Section Eight –
Departmental Stock 125

Index 134

Title Page: 'N' class 2-6-0 No 31862 leaves a rather deserted looking Tunbridge Wells West with an Eastbourne or Brighton-Tonbridge and onwards to Redhill/Guildford/Reading train (possibly the 7.55am from Brighton which was a through service to Reading as the head code onward from Tonbridge is already carried) in April 1964, comprising two Maunsell restriction 1 half-sets type E. These were originally four-coach formations of two brake thirds and two composites, but by 1962 all were already over 30 years old and withdrawals had started. This led to a shortage of restriction 1 stock in the Tonbridge/Tunbridge Wells area so the decision was taken to split all those remaining in half to cover the services. If two sets were available, they would be used, but some trains would have to make do with just one set – with consequent overcrowding. Set numbers allocated were 180-192, 217-219 and 444-467, and some of these continued to run between Eastbourne, Brighton, Tunbridge Wells, Tonbridge, Redhill and Reading until early in 1965. The two sets in the train are formed with the brake coaches inwards, while the leading composite has acquired the yellow first-class band that had begun to be applied in 1962. Another identical set may also be seen in the bay platform. Pages 47-49 give more details. Bulleid three-sets 83 and 84 stand in the carriage sidings on the left – both were four-sets until 1962. Formations of these are:

Set 83: brake thirds Nos 4017/18 and composite No 5826;

Set 84: Brake thirds Nos 4019/20 and composite No 5827.

Until 1962, each set included a corridor third coupled adjacent to the lower numbered brake – these vehicles were Nos 29 and 30 respectively. As four-sets they had begun life in 1949 on Kent coast services but only set No 84 lasted long enough to finish its days on SW section services from Waterloo. Note that the far brake coach in set No 83 has been reversed and faces inwards. All third-class compartments had, of course, been restyled second class from June 1956 and this applies to all carriage stock captions throughout this book. *R Hobbs*

Introduction

This is the third in my series of Southern colour albums and, as the title implies, will cover all the subject areas from the first two books: namely wagons, vans and coaches, together with some subjects hitherto omitted, including milk tanks, special cattle wagons and some departmental stock. At present it is anticipated that this will be the last volume in the series for the foreseeable future – unless of course some new cache of material appears from an unexpected source – and, from recent experience, one cannot discount this possibility, but what is included here has now almost exhausted the supply of material to hand.

I have once again been fortunate in enlisting the help of a number of photographers who had the foresight to put a colour film in their cameras during the 1950s/1960s/1970s and record for posterity scenes that we could previously only enjoy in black and white – and I am grateful to them all. I would especially like to mention Mike Rhodes, Roy Hobbs, Roy Denison, Rodney Lissenden (for providing yet another selection of slides taken by the late Dick Riley), Martin Gill, David Wigley, Peter Fidczuk, David Gould, Don Rowland, Geoff Kent, Terry Cole, Kevin Robertson, Roger Hardingham, Nick Pomfret, George Reeve and finally Ted Crawforth, who has again looked up construction and withdrawal dates of, in particular, milk tanks and goods wagons.

Finally, a round-up of small additions and corrections from the first two volumes, as follows:

Southern Wagons in Colour

Plate 100 – Numbers of the four rebuilt Diagram 1541 vans were 56044/46-48, not as printed.

Plate 140 – Location is Reading, not Taunton.

Southern Vans & Coaches in Colour

The cover picture at Bramshott Halt, together with **Plates 60, 99 and 121** were taken by Trevor Owen.

Plate 66 – The ex-SR number of DS1450 was 4670, not 4760 as printed.

Plate 114 – 'Under the wall' was a description taken from the SR station diagram and may have no connection with the Army in regard to the origin of the name.

Plate 116 – Location is Guildford, not Clapham Junction.

Plate 118 – The 'short' working to Guildford returned from Baynards at 9.46am.

Plates 144 and 145 – The SR numbers quoted in the final three lines of the caption should read 7877 and 7874 respectively, not 7677 and 7877 as printed.

My apologies for these – my fault entirely! Thanks are due to Mike Rhodes and David Gould for pointing them out.

Mike King,
Woking,
September 2015

Pre-Grouping Passenger Stock

An ex-LSWR arc-roofed 34ft six-wheeled six-compartment third now in the ownership of the Swanage Railway, seen on the loading dock at Corfe Castle in August 1978 – the first item of 'rolling stock' purchased by the railway, arriving there on 8 May 1976. Recovered from a garden at Highcliffe, near Christchurch, this was one of at least 173 such vehicles built for the LSWR between 1882 and 1886 – referred to in the minutes as 'large thirds' for fairly obvious reasons! This one was LSWR No 695, dating from 1885 and was almost certainly formed in a set of coaches for use on SW London suburban trains into and out of Waterloo. In December 1904 it was ciphered, ie relegated to the duplicate list and then numbered 0695, in anticipation of early withdrawal. However, it continued in service, probably on some LSWR country branch line, until 1921 when finally withdrawn and the body sold off. Perhaps as few as nine such third class coaches became SR duplicate stock in 1923 and the last of these was withdrawn three years later, while four more were converted to fruit vans and managed to survive until September 1930, probably all still in LSWR livery to the end.

Once in preservation No 0695 was soon painted in a 'pseudo' LSWR livery but one compartment door had been replaced by a more conventional domestic door during private ownership and, as the other doors were all sealed up, this has been retained. The vehicle has been used as a store and been repositioned at least twice – its current location is on the trackside opposite Swanage loco shed. The long-term aim is to mount the body on a suitable underframe and return it to passenger-carrying condition, being one of several such coach bodies acquired by the Swanage Railway for this eventual purpose. *M Rhodes*

One of the 56ft four-compartment brake thirds built for four-coach 'cross-country' sets between 1904 and 1910, to SR Diagram 124, seen awaiting the call to Newhaven for scrapping, at Polegate on 13 June 1965. It has clearly seen better days and even the former identity has been painted out from its very faded and peeling crimson lake livery. Built as LSWR No 629 in October 1909, it was renumbered 1789 as part of the LSWR 1912 renumbering scheme, although this did not actually take place until March 1915. At Grouping it was allocated the SR number 2990 and set 141 (the LSWR set number might have been 58, although this is not known for certain), but SR renumbering did not actually take place until 5 June 1926. The other coaches in the set were companion brake third No 2968 (LSWR No 1486), Diagram 17 all-third No 619 (LSWR No 865 – see *Southern Vans & Coaches in Colour* Plate 5 for details of a similar vehicle) and Diagram 274 composite No 5068 (LSWR No 3098 – see page 8 in this volume). The former LSWR post-1912 numbers are given in brackets. The set continued to run on South Western section stopping and semi-fast duties until about 1931, when it was increased to seven coaches for excursion and special traffic, having 46ft first No 7129 and two 48ft composites – Nos 4678 and 4723 – added in the centre of the set.

Two examples of its workings in this form were on Sunday 20 September 1931, when it formed the 10.23am Reading to Bognor Regis excursion and, three days later, a similar 10.17am Reading to Brighton excursion, both probably routed via Cranleigh with reversal at Christ's Hospital. It remained as a seven-set until sometime after September 1932, when it was further increased to 10 coaches by the addition of 48ft eight-compartment thirds Nos 320, 330 and 442. Then renumbered as 'long' set 324, it was now based at Walton-on-Thames (Oatlands) sidings and continued to be used for excursion traffic, mostly originating from south-west London and Surrey suburban stations until sometime in 1936, when it was returned to its original four-coach formation. Soon after this, in August 1937, third No 619 was removed as part of a reorganisation of SW Section stock and, now as three-set 324 it continued to be used on SW section local services until withdrawn in May 1956. In May 1958 coach No 2990 was taken into internal use by the Operating Department as a store at Blackheath, renumbered 080679, where it remained in static use until withdrawn in March 1965. *R Hobbs*

Two more Diagram 124 brake thirds that managed to stay together even after transfer to departmental stock. Redhill breakdown train riding vans Nos DS1905/6 are seen at the shed in July 1962, freshly repainted in bright red – the usual colour for breakdown vehicles at that time. Both were built in December 1907, as LSWR Nos 1458 and 1457 respectively – retaining these numbers until after the Grouping and running at each end of a four-coach 'cross-country' set; however, the exact LSWR number of this is unknown. They were repainted and renumbered as SR Nos 2959/58 on 16 July 1927, along with Diagram 17 third No 613 and Diagram 274 composite No 5064, as SR set No 133. This was reduced to three coaches (minus third No 613) in June 1938, being withdrawn in January 1943 – although the set was actually deleted from carriage working notices two years earlier. The composite was later grounded at Horsham but the two brake thirds became Nos 1905/6s at Redhill shed in November 1943, where they remained until replaced by a pair of 'Ironclad' conversions in 1963 – not long before the shed closed to steam.

The two replacements are seen on page 11. Coach No DS1906 was noted and photographed by Mike Rhodes in use as a mess room at Bournemouth East Goods in September 1965 – still labelled Redhill Breakdown Train – by which time the paint finish had deteriorated considerably. Withdrawal for this coach is recorded as February 1966. *R Hobbs (both)*

Southern Rolling Stock in Colour

One – Pre-Grouping Passenger Stock

Opposite top: The companion 56ft lavatory composite coaches in the four-coach 'cross-country' sets were to SR Diagram 274, originally with two third-class and five first-class compartments. When the sets were reduced to three coaches, two more compartments were downgraded to third, resulting in the diagram number being amended to 274A. Camping coach No W31S is seen not long after purchase by the Kent & East Sussex Railway at Robertsbridge on 27 October 1968. The two original third-class compartments are nearest the camera, while the two downgraded ones are at the far end. Originally all first-class compartments except that at the far end had access to a lavatory.

Built as LSWR No 959 in December 1907, it was renumbered to 3078 as late as February 1919 (a very late post-1912 renumbering), becoming SR No 5065 on 10 January 1925, now in SR set No 134 along with Diagram 124 brake thirds Nos 2960/61 (LSWR Nos 1459/60) and Diagram 17 third No 614 (LSWR No 855). This ran as a four-set until July 1937, when coach No 614 was removed, then as a three-set until withdrawn in March 1953. Coach No 5065 was converted to camping coach No 31 in time for the 1954 season, serving at Amberley for a number of years before going to Bere Ferrers (Devon) in 1962, just in time to be passed into Western Region ownership in January 1963 – hence the 'W' prefix to the number. The Western Region ceased operating camping coaches after the 1964 season and the coach was later noted in departmental use at Swindon, Kensington Addison Road and Southall, before transfer to the KESR in September 1968. There only limited restoration was carried out and it served for many years as a carriage & wagon department store. Its present status is not known. *D Wigley*

Opposite bottom: Two ex-LSWR coaches at a most unlikely location – the former LNWR carriage works at Wolverton – on 4 May 1969. The writer can confirm that they were still there in the following September and that they were finally broken up in March 1970. They were former camping coaches Nos 34 (Diagram 274 composite No 5049 – nearest) and 35 (Diagram 280 corridor composite No 5108 – farthest) and had previously been stored at Birmingham Moor Street station. As such they were illustrated and described fully in *Southern Vans & Coaches in Colour,* Plate 14. Both were modified as camping coaches in early 1954 and deployed at East Budleigh on the Tipton St Johns-Exmouth loop line. They were retired from these duties after the 1964 season and both coaches were then collected together, along with two other ex-SR and four Pullman camping coaches, at Exmouth for departmental redeployment on the Western Region. This ultimately took them to West Midlands locations, where a further regional boundary change saw them pass into London Midland Region ownership, becoming their internal user vehicles 021801/2 respectively, which is how they came to end up at Wolverton. They were inspected for possible preservation but were then considered not worth saving. Final withdrawal occurred in August 1969. *D Wigley*

Below: Another ex-LSWR coach in an unlikely location. This is former camping coach No 32 at Worcester, by now renumbered as WR departmental permanent way staff & tool van DW150383, in 1975. By now it carries WR departmental black livery and remained in use until October 1978. Built in November 1918 as LSWR 56ft corridor brake composite No 3651, it was one of a very small number of high-roofed LSWR timber-panelled coaches – most had the lower semi-elliptical roof profile – and this may be seen to advantage in this view. It became SR No 6538 on 14 February 1925 – the date on which it received SR Maunsell green livery and it ran as a loose coach allocated to through traffic between West Country branches and Waterloo. By the late 1940s these duties had passed to more modern Maunsell and Bulleid vehicles so it saw out its days on various branch lines, including Exmouth and Torrington-Halwill. Withdrawn in February 1953, it was converted into camping coach No 32 in March 1954, then being allocated to Martin Mill in Kent, moving westward again to Wrafton in 1962, passing into WR ownership with the regional boundary changes of January 1963. It then moved to Swindon and then Bristol, where it was pictured in Plate 27 of *Southern Vans & Coaches in Colour* before moving on to its final destination of Worcester in 1966. *M Rhodes*

Pull-push set No 1 during its foray to the west of England from its usual Hampshire haunts – at Seaton Junction, where it served for a few months, *circa* August 1961. It was also seen at Yeovil Town before moving to Tunbridge Wells West, from where the set was withdrawn in July 1962. It is in its final form as running after July 1958 – the coaches being LSWR 56ft driving brake composite No 6488 (Diagram 419) and SECR 60ft 1in 'long ten' No 1066 (Diagram 52). Full details of these are given with Plates 15 and 60 in *Southern Vans & Coaches in Colour*. In its previous formation it had been repainted from SR malachite to BR crimson lake in October 1951 and was returned to Southern Region green in August 1960. Note the dimension, tare weight and route restriction plates (in this instance, surprisingly, Restriction 1) are obvious on the driving end, with the lettering picked out in yellow paint.

The single route disc correctly signifies the Seaton branch, although on this day the set was not in use – Maunsell set No 603 was on duty. Several milk tank wagons are seen behind – there was an Express Dairy depot on the up side, behind the station platform. Contrary to what one might expect, pull-push operation was not very common in the west of England, with only the Yeovil Town, Seaton and Turnchapel branches being regularly operated as such. Other seemingly likely routes, such as Lyme Regis, Sidmouth, Tipton St Johns-Exmouth, Callington and Bodmin were excluded, owing to either sharp curves, steep gradients or the need for more flexible operation due to wide variations in traffic levels. Surprisingly, pull-push was much more common in Dorset, Hampshire and the Home Counties. *G W Powell, courtesy The South Western Circle*

Opposite top: One more view of ex-LSWR 'Longmoor Saloon' No WD3007 at Longmoor Downs station on the June 1967 annual open day – again showing the absolutely magnificent finish maintained by the Army for its three VIP saloons and a far cry from the present state of this particular vehicle. The LSWR bequeathed at least 26 saloon coaches to the Southern in 1923 – mostly for first-class private hire – but there were some third-class 'picnic' saloons amongst this total. Demand for such vehicles waned considerably in the first quarter of the 20th century and it must seem strange that this type of traffic could have once been so lucrative for the railways – so different to the 'one size fits all' thinking that prevails today. Full details of this coach was given with Plate 31 of *Southern Vans & Coaches in Colour* so will not be repeated here. *M Rhodes*

Opposite bottom: A general view of Redhill shed, taken in June 1965, just prior to 'actual' closure. Official closure had taken place six months earlier when the Reading-Redhill line was passed over to diesel traction but, as may be seen, steam continued to be serviced there for a while to come – BR standard Class 4 tanks being much in evidence and a number may be seen, plus a Southern mogul. Also visible are the LSWR 'Ironclad' breakdown riding vans, replacements for the earlier coaches seen on page 7. These are tool van No DS70127 (nearest) and staff van No DS70123 (farthest from the camera). Both were considerably rebuilt from their former corridor third-class configurations in November 1963 and were part of a general upgrade of breakdown

One – Pre-Grouping Passenger Stock

vans throughout the Southern Region. No DS70127 was ex-third LSWR No 70, built to the designs of Surrey Warner, Carriage & Wagon Superintendent, in June 1923 for Bournemouth line five-set No 7c, later SR set No 437, with eight compartments and a lavatory at each end, to SR Diagram 24. It did appear in LSWR green livery when new, being renumbered to SR 726 on 10 November 1928, along with the other four coaches in the set. Later the coach was transferred to similar set No 435 and, by the late 1950s, was in use for Bertram Mills Circus train.

Withdrawn in August 1959, it stood around for some time before being rebuilt into the form seen here, almost devoid of windows and with two sets of large sliding doors on each side. No DS70123 was slightly newer and was completed in April 1924 as a loose coach for Bournemouth line services, not being allocated a pre-Grouping number. Eventually it was formed in sets Nos 441 and later 440 before being withdrawn in July 1959. Rather less modified for its new role, it retains most windows on each side. Both coaches were later moved to Horsham, where in 1976 they were taken into internal user stock and renumbered 083233/34 respectively. *R Hobbs*

Closer views of two 'Ironclad' breakdown unit staff vans – almost identical vehicles converted to drawing No W850, although there are some detail differences. No DS172 is seen from the compartment side at Eastleigh in the late 1960s and is one of the earlier Diagram 23 vehicles with Warner double-framed 'Dreadnought' bogies. This was built as pantry third LSWR No 930 in July 1921, for Bournemouth line five-set No 1c, having a lavatory at one end, then seven third-class compartments and a small pantry at the other, capable of serving teas and light refreshments only. Only the first four 'Ironclad' sets (Nos 1c-4c, later SR Nos 431-434) featured these, but they were not repeated in the 10 later sets. The pantry compartment was at the end farthest from the camera, but there is now nothing visible to indicate this.

In February 1924 the coach, along with the rest of the set, was repainted in SR livery, this coach becoming SR No 713 in set No 431. The pantry clearly proved too small for most requirements, so in March 1927 was enlarged at the expense of the adjacent third-class compartment. In this form the coach was used as a loose light catering vehicle, mostly on Weymouth or Swanage through trains or on Southampton boat services. In July 1936 it was again rebuilt into an almost conventional eight-compartment corridor third, then being reformed into several of the 'Ironclad' sets numbered between 431 and 444 until withdrawn in April 1957, finally being rebuilt into the form seen here.

Similar vehicle No DS230 from Hither Green shed is seen from the corridor side at Streatham Common on 8 March 1965, while attending a goods train derailment, also seen again in page 133. This was a slightly newer coach, completed in May 1924 as SR No 753 – an eight-compartment third to Diagram 24 from the same batch as No DS70123 seen on page 11 and instead has 9ft wheelbase 'VS' bogies. Again at first a loose strengthening coach for Bournemouth and Portsmouth services, this was later incorporated into 'Ironclad' eight-set No 437 from about 1948 until withdrawn in August 1959, before being converted into breakdown riding van No DS230 in January 1960. The companion tool van, No DS229 just creeps into shot at right; this was to the same windowless pattern as No DS70127 at Redhill. In all these conversions, the rather lighter underframe trussing has been replaced by heavy 'L' angle trussing mounted outside the solebars to allow the coaches to carry much heavier breakdown equipment. *NB collection/M W F Gill*

One – Pre-Grouping Passenger Stock

'Ironclad' four-compartment brake third No DS70085 at Yeovil Junction on 10 February 1973, showing the corridor side. The compartment side was illustrated in Plate 33 of *Southern Vans & Coaches in Colour*, so the full history will not be repeated here. Because this side faced north, it has retained its green livery in a rather better state. However, it does show an 'Ironclad' almost in passenger running condition instead of modified for departmental purposes. Although this coach was a departmental – allocated to the Engineer's as a staff van – it was almost unique in retaining its gangway connections and was almost unaltered externally on transfer. It was a great pity that, once purchased for preservation, it was allowed to deteriorate so far that it had to be broken up.

This picture also shows the original style of underframe truss rodding. The 14 longer 'Ironclad' sets on the SW section (Nos 431-444) were used on the best Bournemouth, Weymouth, Portsmouth and some west of England services from new until displaced by Maunsell stock in the early/mid-1930s. They then moved onto secondary duties, such as Brighton-Bournemouth and Portsmouth-Bristol and Cardiff trains until relegated to excursion, inter-regional and more seasonal trains after 1948. Many set formation changes were made; although most were initially five-coach formations, these could often be increased to six, seven or eight vehicles or reduced to four as occasion and services demanded. After 1948, most were lengthened to eight coaches, which is how they remained until withdrawn between 1957 and 1961. Some have lasted as long in departmental stock as they did in passenger service! *D Wigley*

The five two-coach 'Ironclad' sets allocated to the SW section (sets Nos 381-385) were used mostly for through portions from Waterloo to Lymington, Swanage and, to a lesser extent, to West Country branches until rebuilt as pull-push sets between 1948 and 1952. Shortly after 2pm on 15 August 1959 'M7' No 30058 and set No 382, with an ex-SECR 'air control van' unusually on the rear of the train (it ought to be between the locomotive and the set), pass Lymington Junction with a Bournemouth West bound local via Ringwood. Some shunting will be needed on arrival at Bournemouth West, as the van is coupled to the driving end of the pull-push set! The coaches are Diagram 414 brake composite No 6561 leading and Diagram 136 driving brake third No 4053 behind, while the utility van is one of Nos 1996, 2001/2/4/5. This alone appears to be in Southern Region green, while the pull-push set is in crimson lake.

The set was fitted for pull-push operation in July 1949 and was originally allocated to the Gosport branch but by 1959 was on services radiating from Bournemouth, ie Swanage and the 'old road' to Brockenhurst via Wimborne and Ringwood, plus trips down the Lymington branch – where George Powell had photographed it earlier that day. It suffered fire damage at Bournemouth West just five days later and was condemned in October 1959 – the only one of the five sets not to receive Southern Region green livery. *G W Powell, courtesy The South Western Circle*

One – Pre-Grouping Passenger Stock

Former 'Ironclad' restaurant car No DS625, photographed from the other end and at the other side of Guildford station than seen in Plate 39 of *Southern Vans & Coaches in Colour*, in mid-1974, when its departmental olive green livery looked rather more presentable. The first two of these coaches were ordered by the LSWR and delivered in October 1923, carrying their LSWR numbers 4150/51 but already in dark green livery. Repainting into SR colours, therefore, was not difficult, requiring no more than a renumbering and the alteration of the company title, so this was actually done for these two coaches as soon as 31 December 1923 – probably some of the earliest vehicles to receive full SR livery and numbers. No DS625 was formerly LSWR No 4151, later SR No 7851. The other six coaches carried SR lettering and numbers from new, being completed in July and August 1925. They would work turn and turnabout with Maunsell vehicles and could easily find themselves in a set formed otherwise of Maunsell stock, for which purpose they were fitted with Pullman gangway adaptors.

The coach is parked alongside part of the former cattle docks at Guildford. In days gone by, the regular cattle markets held in the town would ensure plenty of activity in the goods yard, but by the 1960s all this had passed into history. *M Rhodes*

Perhaps not the most ideal of views, but an interesting and unique vehicle. This is 26ft four-wheel fruit train passenger brake van LSWR No 46, built in February 1895. It was renumbered to 4362 on 17 December 1913 and became SR van No 1 after the Grouping, although it took until March 1929 to receive this number, to SR Diagram 850. It was the only vehicle of its type and was equipped with louvre ventilators at eaves level down each side, just visible in the photograph. The Southern Railway plated over portions of these to receive the company title and number in the standard positions.

The van was, in effect, similar to a 24ft fruit van but with a guard's compartment added at one end. In April/May 1930 it was renumbered as 1007 and shipped to the Isle of Wight, where it remained until June 1938, usually working between Ryde Pier Head and Ventnor, carrying passenger's luggage – of which there were large quantities on the Island. It then received a further lease of life by being grounded on the trackside at Ryde St Johns for use as a store in December 1938, where it remained until the mid-1960s, being photographed there in 1964. It actually spanned a small stream alongside the line! The body was the usual 8ft 0¾in wide, while the lookouts at the nearer end increased this to 9ft 1in, meaning that the route restriction was 3. The stove chimney was, of course, an addition after being grounded. *M Rhodes*

LSWR 24ft passenger luggage van No DS1686 at Horsted Keynes in the late 1970s and before any restoration work was attempted, still carrying very faded Southern Region green livery. This was one of 204 completed between 1909 and 1923, this example dating from 1920 as LSWR No 5498. It was renumbered as SR No 1584 after the Grouping, to Diagram 929 and would have been used to carry luggage, mail, milk churns, fruit, flowers and any other perishable traffic – the ventilators in the sides and ends ensuring that the contents stayed cool and fresh during transit. This example entered departmental stock in September 1941, renumbered 1686s, becoming a Carriage & Wagon Section mobile charging van – one of a number converted around that time. The four end windows (in this end only) were put in as part of the conversion work. In BR days it became No DS1686 and was allocated to Exeter Central – usually being found parked in the sidings adjacent to the carriage shed on the down side approaching the station.

Passed to Western Region ownership in January 1963, it was condemned at Newton Abbott on 26 June 1969 and sold to the Southern Locomotive Preservation Co at Liss in April 1970. There it was hoped to reopen the former Longmoor Military Railway as a preservation society but, when this failed, the van was moved to the Bluebell Railway, where it arrived in October 1971. Since then, apart from essential protection work, little restoration has been possible. *Author*

Another of the C & W Section mobile charging vans is seen in Tonbridge yard in mid-1967. This was No DS1653, ex-luggage van No 1434 in November 1941 and was originally allocated to Victoria station sidings or Stewarts Lane, moving to Tonbridge yard in the early 1960s. This retains Southern Region green sides, but unusually has dull red-painted ends; proving that where departmental stock was concerned, any livery combination was possible.

Like No DS1686, this also has four windows added to one end. It was one of the original batch to this design, dating from June 1911 as LSWR luggage van No 8, renumbered to 5008 in December 1916. Other identical charging vans were Nos DS1685 and 1687, both of which also survived to the late 1960s. Other items of SR interest visible include a Diagram 1582 25-ton goods brake van in pale grey livery and, in the nearer foreground, a Southern 12-ton covered goods van, identifiable by its characteristic semi-elliptical roof profile. *M Rhodes*

One – Pre-Grouping Passenger Stock

Moving on to ex-SECR stock, we start with 50ft 1in 'Birdcage' six-compartment former brake composite No DS3208, photographed soon after arrival on the Bluebell Railway, at Sheffield Park in May 1962 and before any restoration work was started. It still carries the legend 'M & EE Surbiton' and also the word 'Staff' on its departmental black finish. Built at Ashford Works in December 1909, numbered SECR 1061, it had a single second-class compartment at the far end, followed by five third-class compartments, some six inches narrower than the end compartment, plus a combined guard's/luggage compartment with lookout atop at the nearer end. It was formed at one end of SECR Trio-A 3-coach set No 102 along with 54ft 1in lavatory composite SECR 1034 and 50ft 1in lavatory composite brake SECR No 1047.

These were some of the first of the SECR trio sets, which in various forms (Trio-A, B, C and D) eventually numbered 126 sets and became the backbone of South Eastern main-line services for many years to come. These three coaches became SR set No 541 after the Grouping – although not actually repainted and renumbered to SR livery until January 1929, renumbered as 3334, 5428 and 3352 respectively, to SR Diagrams 155, 314 and 156. Both brake coaches had now been downgraded to third class, as the Southern dispensed with second class on all except a few boat trains. The set remained in traffic until February 1952, being used on South Eastern and, later, Central section 'rover' workings. They were designated as three-sets type R (for rover – as they were used indiscriminately on any duty requiring such a three-set).

After withdrawal both brake coaches entered departmental stock, renumbered as DS3208 and DS3209. The former coach was then used to carry staff engaged on electrical recabling work to and from their site of work, for which purpose all lighting and heating circuits were disconnected, while some internal fitting were removed, but seats and compartment partitions remained in place. Clearly the workers were given only the minimum of comfort! It worked on both the South Eastern and the South Western sections, latterly being based at Surbiton yard (although often working from Esher) and was withdrawn from these duties in September 1961 and purchased for preservation in February 1962. In due course restoration to SECR livery as No 1061 took place and the coach re-entered passenger traffic in June 1965; however, not all the restoration was as thorough as would be attempted nowadays and eventually the vehicle had to be withdrawn pending a very much more extensive overhaul. This has yet to be attempted. The rather attractive Triumph Herald also deserves mention. *R Hobbs*

The next batches of SECR Trio-A sets included all three vehicles at 54ft 1in long over bodywork. Twenty of these were put into service in 1910/11 and became SR set Nos 543-562 after the Grouping. Most of the coaches were rebuilt and shipped to the Isle of Wight during 1948/49 and, as such, will feature in various forms on pages 20-22; however, one set was sold to the Army for use at Longmoor in 1943: SR set No 552.

The history of this set was fully detailed in *Southern Vans & Coaches in Colour* Plate 52, but two more pictures are included here. The top image shows both brake coaches, now numbered WD5311/12, at Longmoor Downs station in May 1965, with seven-compartment brake third No WD5312 (ex-SR No 3388 to Diagram 159) nearest the camera and six-compartment lavatory brake third No WD5311 (ex-SR No 3368 to Diagram 158) farthest from the camera. The bottom image is a close-up of the latter vehicle at Liss on 23 May 1964. This included a single second-class compartment at the far end, then two lavatories serving each adjacent compartment, then five slightly narrower third-class compartments and a guard's/luggage van that was slightly bigger than those included in the very similar 50ft 1in brake coaches.

The solitary second-class compartment was downgraded to third class after 1923. Notice that quite a number of the timber panels have been covered by steel sheeting – this is much more extensive on No WD5311 than No 5312. Whilst most of this work may be attributed to Army carpenters, such a procedure was also regularly carried out by the Southern. The former lavatory window has also been entirely sheeted over – presumably the Army did not require such provision – or at least, did not wish to maintain it! To them, at Longmoor, this was passenger set No 1 as stencilled on the coach end and through the 1950s and 1960s provided most of the regular service personnel trains – latterly having an ex-GWR 'Toplight' coach as the centre vehicle; once the former SECR composite had been scrapped. *R Hobbs/M W F Gill*

One – Pre-Grouping Passenger Stock

An interior view of one of the 'Birdcage' brake compartments at Longmoor, taken on 23 May 1964. This shows the guard's observation platform and seat, reached by three steps and allowing him to view the track and signals while the train was in motion from the comfort of his van. Note also the Westinghouse and vacuum release valves and pressure gauges on the coach end. The Westinghouse equipment was presumably fitted by the Southern Railway prior to purchase by the Army. The hand brake wheel is out of sight to the right, but the ratchet mechanism may be seen on the end of the coach on the previous image. The appropriateness of the 'birdcage' name is also evident. *M W F Gill*

Staying with Longmoor for a moment, this is the other VIP blue saloon, ex-SECR coach Army No WD3006 seen in the yard at Longmoor Downs on 30 April 1966 – the day of the second RCTS Longmoor tour from Waterloo and marked by hot, sunny weather. The writer was on the first a fortnight earlier – in pouring rain! The coach was fully described with Plate 47 in *Southern Vans & Coaches in Colour* but here we are able to appreciate the absolutely pristine condition as well as the still fully panelled sides and ends – and the fact that the VIP set was not Westinghouse fitted but just vacuum braked. The electrical wiring and sockets on the end also show that probably only the ex-LSWR vehicle carried a dynamo and battery boxes for lighting purposes. The SR dimension and tare weight plates are also still in place, with lettering picked out in white. Only the route restriction Plate (it should have been Restriction 0) – if fitted originally – has gone. *M W F Gill*

Now for a small mystery. The 7ft wheelbase Fox pressed steel bogie under SECR Longmoor saloon No 3006. Note, however, that the axle-box covers are cast with the letters LSWR, not SE&CR as might be expected and presumably are not the original fittings. Study of black & white photographs reveals that this change occurred between August 1946 and September 1950 – presumably in the interests of standardisation. Possibly the wheelsets have been changed to LSWR pattern as well, to suit the axle boxes.

The coach in preservation today on the Kent & East Sussex Railway still retains these boxes. 7ft wheelbase bogies were provided on SECR bogie coaches less than 43ft long; 45ft and over used a similar 8ft pattern, but 44ft coaches might be fitted with either type. *M Rhodes*

Haven Street station on 14 August 1965, with '02' No 28 *Ashey* waiting in the loop with a train for Ryde Pier Head as sister engine No 16 *Ventnor* arrives with a Cowes working. Both trains are composed of four coaches – three ex-SECR rebuilds and an ex-LBSCR six- or seven-compartment brake third, which will be at the Cowes end of each set. The SECR brake on the up train, No S4146, began life as Diagram 159 seven-compartment 'Birdcage' brake SR No 3387/SECR No 1105, looking just like WD5312 on page 18. In February 1949 this was taken into Lancing Works for refurbishment for the Isle of Wight. This involved the removal of the 'Birdcage' lookout and the conversion of three passenger compartments into a much-enlarged luggage van – to cater for the considerable volumes of holidaymakers' luggage dealt with on the Island. Notice that almost all of the timber mouldings have been replaced by steel sheeting. Renumbered into the Island series, it arrived in April 1949 to become the Ryde Pier Head end coach of set No 490, to SR Diagram 171.

Because Isle of Wight set formations were nothing like as constant as on the mainland, the coach moved around the sets somewhat and, in summer 1965, was formed at one end of Newport-based set No 485 – the other vehicles being SECR composites Nos 6375 and 6380, with ex-LBSCR six-compartment brake third No 4154 at the other end. The set behind No W16 is likely to be No 487, formed of LBSCR seven-compartment brake No 4160, SECR composite No 6370, SECR third No 2456 and SECR brake third No 4137. For the Newport and Cowes line this was to be its last summer, as closure to passengers occurred on the following 21 February, leaving just goods traffic from Medina Wharf to run through Haven Street. Coach No 4146 was withdrawn from service the very same day, as were all the others noted, except for composite No 6375, which lasted to the end of steam operation and was then purchased for preservation by the Isle of Wight steam railway (see page 21). *MBW collection*

Opposite top: Diagram 171 SECR rebuilt brake third No S4135 (island stock never carried the 'S' suffix letter) in the sidings at Ryde St Johns on 21 July 1963. Formerly Diagram 159 'Birdcage' brake third SECR No 1103/SR No 3385, dating from December 1910, this ran in Trio-A set SECR No 115/SR set No 554 until May 1948, when it was rebuilt into the form illustrated. On arrival in the Isle of Wight, it was formed in three-set No 495, along with SECR Diagram 378 composite No 6371 and LBSCR Diagram 210 six-compartment brake third No 4163. For just how long this formation was maintained is not known, but from 1959 until 1963 it was at the Ryde end of set No 493 – a six-coach summer formation for the Ventnor line. In June 1960, it was specifically noted as still painted in early BR crimson lake livery. By the date of the picture, it was still in this set, but clearly now in Southern Region green.

By 1965, however, it was included in set No 491. Note that most of the passenger compartment section still retains timber panelling, while much of the guard's van (ie the rebuilt portion) is steel sheeted. Just before the end, probably early in 1966, the

passenger compartment adjacent to the luggage van was converted into a mail compartment – presumably by removal of seating. Most of the surviving Diagram 171 vehicles were so altered at this time, but it is not believed a new diagram number was issued. Withdrawal is recorded as 24 September 1966, breaking up taking place two months later. *R Hobbs*

One of the companion ex-SECR 54ft 1in composite rebuilds; this is Diagram 378X former composite 6375 – by now demoted to all third (second) class for the final year of steam operation. The picture was taken on 8 October 1966 at Ryde St Johns Road.

This coach began life as SECR lavatory composite No 1133 in December 1911, then with four first-and three second-class compartments, plus two lavatories in the centre, serving each adjacent first-class compartment. The former seconds were the two nearest and the one at the far end. These became third class on entering SR ownership. Included as the centre coach in SECR Trio-A set No 108, this became SR set No 547 on repainting in Southern livery, which took place on 25 July 1927, when the coach received the new number 5412, to SR Diagram 313.

The set continued to run on South Eastern and Central section 'rover' workings until 1948. In March 1949 the coach entered Lancing Works for rebuilding; this involved removal of the lavatories and knocking these into the two compartments on either side, to produce a large saloon – here occupying the third and fourth compartments from the left-hand end, plus the portion of the former lavatories, now with a single glazed window between these 'compartments'. Although all 18 conversions were structurally the same, there were at least four different diagrams allocated depending on the number and position of the first-class compartments. Three of the coaches became all third vehicles on transfer to the Island, to SR Diagram 41 (Nos 2456-58, with seats for 70 passengers). Coach No 6375 arrived on the Island on 13 April 1949 and was a Diagram 378 composite, with the saloon and the compartment to its right allocated to first-class passengers. The saloon seated 16 passengers in four runs of four – two running longitudinally below the former lavatory windows. This diagram was amended to 378X (a mnemonic for ex-Diagram 378!) when reduced to all second early in 1966, although in fact this was the second use of the diagram number for these coaches on the Island – it had previously indicated a coach where the saloon was all third but three other compartments were first class. Diagram 376 was for similar coaches with just a first-class saloon (seating 18 passengers) while 377 was for a coach with 18 first-class seats in the saloon, plus one more first-class compartment, so just about every combination was catered for. Add to this the fact that some coaches were altered while on the Island and the result is confusion all round!

Coach No 6375 may have run mostly as a loose strengthening vehicle but was recorded in set No 496 in 1950, No 488 in 1962/63, in set No 485 during 1965 (see page 20) and finally in set No 500 for the last months of steam operation in 1966. It lasted until January 1967, then being saved for preservation by the Isle of Wight Steam Railway and is currently awaiting attention to bogies and underframe at Haven Street. *R Denison*

'O2' tank No 24 *Calbourne* hauls a one-van parcels train towards Smallbrook Junction on 6 August 1966 – note that the locomotive is in unlined black and has replica metal-strip nameplates. The van is one of the four Diagram 891 rebuilds of ex-SECR four-compartment brake thirds. This is No S1013, previously Diagram 171 brake No 4138; rebuilt in September 1956, it ran until 19 November 1966, when all four of these conversions were withdrawn. Almost all timber mouldings were replaced by steel sheeting during the rebuilding – compare with van No 1015 illustrated in *Southern Vans & Coaches in Colour* Plate 54. This view shows a van from the opposite side and end – the latter retaining its timber mouldings. *R Hobbs*

One – Pre-Grouping Passenger Stock

We now come to the 60ft 1in 'Birdcage' stock. In terms of trio sets these were the most numerous and, out of a total of 126 sets, no less than 72 were formed using 60ft 1in vehicles – Trio-C in SECR parlance. They were also the longest lasting with SR sets Nos 592 and 620 being the final survivors in three-coach form, withdrawn in October 1958.

Coach No DS130 is a breakdown mess and tool van allocated to Ashford, photographed there on 14 April 1960 – in the usual bright red livery for breakdown riding vans. Built by Cravens of Sheffield in November 1913 as SECR No 1251, it was formed at one end of trio set SECR No 178 as a composite lavatory brake vehicle, having two second-class compartments at the far end, then a pair of lavatories side by side followed by five third-class compartments and a combined guard's and luggage compartment surmounted by the usual 'birdcage' lookout. One lavatory could be accessed from both second-class compartments while the other was accessible from three of the third-class compartments via short side corridors – not that this was very apparent externally. The companion vehicles in set No 178 were lavatory composite No 1261 and eight-compartment brake third No 1271. These became SR set No 610, renumbered on 23 October 1928; individual coaches becoming SR Nos 3515 (the lavatory composite brake – now brake third to SR Diagram 162), No 5479 (the lavatory composite to SR Diagram 316) and No 3443 (the eight-compartment brake to SR Diagram 160) respectively.

The companion coach types are illustrated below and overleaf. The set continued to serve on 'rover' workings until withdrawn in March 1956. Coach No 3515 was then converted in November 1956 into breakdown van No DS130 for Ashford, remaining in use until April 1966. It was last seen – not looking quite this presentable – at Andover Junction on 14 August 1966 in a line of other condemned 'Birdcage' stock, probably en route to a scrap merchant. *E Hunt, courtesy P Fidczuk*

Identical Diagram 162 coach No DS136 in use as a mobile soil mechanics laboratory at Wimbledon on 22 November 1966, wearing olive green livery. Another coach built by Cravens, this time in August 1913, this was formerly SECR No 1247 and ran at one end of Trio-C set No 174, along with composite No 1257 and brake third No 1267. These three became SR set No 606 on 22 April 1926, coach numbers becoming 3511, 5475 and 3439 to Diagrams 162, 316 and 160 respectively. This remained in service until April 1956, after which No 3511 assumed the identity No DS136 in January 1958. Soil mechanics is a science concerned with such matters as drainage, bearing capacity of the ground, angle of repose of cutting slopes, etc, and so would be of concern on the railway, especially where difficult terrain was encountered, hence the 'Not to be loose shunted' instruction on the end – the coach would contain delicate instruments of measurement which might not take kindly to heavy buffing shocks.

In the picture we are now looking at the end with the two former second-class compartments nearest. Withdrawal date for this coach is not known – but probably relatively recent compared to others. *M W F Gill*

The equivalent 60ft 1in eight-compartment brake third was to SR Diagram 160. This is departmental coach No DS33 as it was delivered to the Bluebell Railway in August 1982, seen at Horsted Keynes on 24 June 1984, in very faded olive green livery – indeed almost a purple-grey colour! Built at Ashford Works in June 1912 as SECR No 1170, it was formed at one end of Trio-C set No 149, along with lavatory composite No 1156 and lavatory composite brake No 1163. Repainted in SR livery on 12 June 1928 (a fairly late repaint), they received the new numbers 3410 (Diagram 160), 5439 (Diagram 315) and 3482 (Diagram 162) respectively, now forming set No 581 and were included in the usual three-set 'R' pool. The set ran until May 1954, after which No 3410 was converted into carriage & wagon examiners instructional coach No DS33, the conversion being completed in January 1956.

After moving around the Southern Region somewhat, the coach eventually entered static internal use at Clapham Junction, renumbered as No 083180 in December 1974. It was purchased subsequently by the Bluebell Railway, arriving there on 1 August 1982. As yet no major restoration has been attempted – but as the railway now has several examples of SECR 'birdcage' stock it must be hoped that soon sufficient coaches are restored to enable a complete South Eastern train to be run. *D Wigley*

One – Pre-Grouping Passenger Stock

A view of Cedar Sidings at Newhaven Harbour on 10th August 1963 – where a great many Southern coaches and wagons met their end. A 1925 South Eastern section electric unit, No 4342, is being broken up and strong men are wielding sledgehammers to it – no doubt a sight to shock any modern health and safety expert! On the left are two grounded vehicle bodies and these may be identified further. The bogie coach is Diagram 316 60ft 1in ex-SECR saloon lavatory composite SR No 5465, formerly SECR No 1213, built by Metropolitan in October 1913 – the centre coach of Trio-C set SECR No 160. This is one of the type with just one large saloon window – Diagram 315 was identical but featured two large windows. For a better illustration of the diagram, see *Southern Vans & Coaches in Colour* Plate 58. No 5465 was grounded here after withdrawal in October 1958, having been in SR set No 592 – one of the final two Trio-C sets in use – and was probably serving as an office for the breaking up gang. At least they would have had the comforts of the former first-class saloon to relax in! The other vehicle to left is LSWR Diagram 929 24ft luggage van No 1609 – which had been grounded here during World War 2. Scrapping of stock finally ceased at this location around mid-1965 – after that time most vehicles were sold to contractors for breaking up. *R C Riley, courtesy Rodney Lissenden*

On 27 October 1963 a rail tour was operated from Brighton to the Bluebell Railway, using the Lancing Works staff train. Entitled 'The Brighton Bluebell', it is seen between Horsted Keynes and Sheffield Park, hauled by 'P' class 0-6-0 No 323 carrying black livery and the name *Bluebell*. Most of the coaches visible are SECR 60ft 1in 'long tens' but the leading brake is No DS70080; this was ex-SECR Trio-C Diagram 161 No 3473. The last 10 Trio-C sets differed from all the rest by having steel-sheeted sides (but not the ends, which remained traditionally covered by timber mouldings) and no 'Birdcage' lookout, making them very obviously different to what had gone before.

The question of lookout provision had been discussed between the SECR General Manager, Francis Dent, Superintendent of Operation, Edwin Cox and their CME, Harry Wainwright, since July 1913. The general consensus was that they were no longer necessary provided end windows were incorporated into the brake vans and the guard's accommodation re-arranged accordingly. Wainwright departed Ashford somewhat under a cloud at the end of 1913 and it fell to his successors, Richard Maunsell and Lionel Lynes, to enact the proposal.

With new brooms at the helm, this was clearly not difficult and these last 10 sets, completed in small batches between 1915 and 1921, reflected the new ideas. Otherwise, the coaches were identical in plan, if not in construction, to the 62 earlier Trio-Cs. No 3473 was built as SECR No 1366 in March 1921, along with lavatory composite No 1363 (later SR No 5502) and lavatory composite brake No 1369 (later SR No 3545) – one of the final three trio sets built before Grouping. SECR set No 204 was allocated, becoming SR set No 636 on repainting, which took place on 30 April 1926. No new diagram number was allocated to the composite, as this differed not at all from the previous panelled vehicles to Diagram 316, but the brake coaches did have new SR diagrams allocated, owing to the lack of the birdcage. These were 161 for the eight-compartment coach, 163 for the seven-compartment lavatory composite brake. Set No 636 joined the usual three-set 'rover' pool until 1955, when it was augmented to six and later seven coaches for special traffic. In this form it was actually the final ex-SECR non-corridor set in traffic, apart from some pull-push units, when it was withdrawn in July 1959. At that time the Lancing Works train comprised a set of ancient LSWR 'short' non-corridors and was due for replacement. In late 1959/early 1960 this was provided using ex-SECR 60ft 1in thirds, some ex-LSWR 58ft rebuild thirds and two ex-LSWR 'Ironclad' brake coaches – the latter numbered DS70061/68. However, coach No 3208/DS70061 was withdrawn almost immediately and No 3473/DS70080 substituted in March 1960. It continued to run in the train until August 1964. *R Hobbs*

Opposite bottom: Coaches in store at Hassocks in August 1963 – another regular location to find parked condemned stock at that time. These are, just seen on the left, SECR 60ft 1in Diagram 52 'long ten' No 1070, in the centre similar but rather faded coach No 1056 and, on the right, Maunsell Diagram 2666 buffet car No 7870. The Diagram 52 vehicles were both part of a batch of 100-seat thirds built by Birmingham RCW Co on underframes supplied by Gloucester RCW Co in August 1921 and were SECR Nos 1388/74 respectively and intended for early conversion to electric stock trailers as part of the then embryo South Eastern's proposed third-/fourth-rail electrification scheme. This failed to happen and the Southern later modified the stock provision somewhat, converting instead some older 46ft thirds to electric stock.

Coach No 1056 ran in various South Eastern section 'long' sets, including (briefly) set No 528 and then No 903 from at least 1931 until 1957. It was equipped for pull-push operation in February 1958 and spent the rest of its life allocated to Tunbridge Wells West as a strengthening coach – mostly on Oxted and Three Bridges services. It was withdrawn in July 1961. Coach No 1070 had a similar history, running in 'long' sets Nos 905 and later 335. After 1956 it was noted as a spare coach on the Bentley-Bordon branch – despite never being pull-push fitted – and then as a loose non-corridor vehicle allocated to the Southern operating district – most likely in the Eastleigh/Southampton/Portsmouth area until 1959, moving to the Oxted line until withdrawn in September 1961. It was actually purchased by the Bluebell Railway but was returned as it had many broken windows – that organisation receiving coach No 1098 in its place (see next picture). Maunsell buffet car No 7870 was originally a restaurant first to SR Diagram 2650, completed in July 1932 but was rebuilt to a Diagram 2666 buffet car in February 1954. In this form it ran until December 1962. *R Hobbs*

'M7' No 30328 with 'Ironclad' pull-push set No 384 and loose strengthener No 1098 stand between Lymington branch duties in Brockenhurst up yard on 15 August 1959. No 1098 is another Diagram 52 SECR 'long ten' and is one of the much more austere looking vehicles built at Ashford Works on underframes supplied by BRCW Co between November 1922 and June 1923 – the last batch of non-corridor coaches ordered by the SECR. SR numbers for these were 968-974 and 1094-1112. They were typified by their complete lack of timber mouldings, including the ends (unlike coaches Nos 1056/70 seen in the previous picture) and very square-shaped window frames. No 1098 was completed in November 1922 as SECR No 1416, at first running as a loose coach but later included for some of its life in 'long' eight-set No 918, based at Grove Park. In February 1943 it was through piped for pull-push working and sent to the SW section – being allocated to the Lymington branch –where it remained, from all appearances, until withdrawn in December 1962 and purchased by the Bluebell Railway from the Ardingly dump, arriving there on 2 May 1963.

Here it is in BR crimson lake but was returned to traffic in Southern Region green livery on 12 May 1961. 'Ironclad' pull-push set No 384 comprises trailer brake composite No 6563 and driving brake third No 3212, running as a pull-push formation from June 1949 until December 1962. This was repainted in Southern Region green livery in January 1961. *G W Powell, courtesy The South Western Circle*

Ex-SECR Post Office van No 4954 at Eardley Road carriage sidings (Streatham) on 30 October 1960. This is a 50ft 1in long vehicle to SR Diagram 1207 but was actually built as a non-gangwayed bogie stowage/luggage van in April 1907, SECR No 110. Five were built at that time, primarily for traffic between London-Folkestone and Dover – SECR numbers being 110-114 – and these usually, but not exclusively ran with the various SECR GPO sorting vans. They became SR luggage vans Nos 2018-22, to Diagram 961 after the Grouping. Vans Nos 2021/22 remained unaltered but Nos 2018-20 were converted to dedicated GPO stowage vans in October 1931, renumbered as 4954-56.

In this form they were not all the same, as Nos 4954/55 had a lavatory provided (Diagram 1207) while No 4956 did not (Diagram 1208). The lavatory was on the far side, at the far end, and was provided with an obscured window on the other side of the van. Offset gangway connections were fitted to all three vans on conversion. In this form they continued to run on South Eastern section mail trains between Cannon Street, London Bridge and Dover or Charing Cross and Dover via Redhill but, by 1935, van No 4954 was in use on the former LBSCR service to Newhaven Harbour, running from Holborn Viaduct via East Croydon. All continental mail services were suspended during World War 2 and the coaches were stored in the ample sidings at Epsom Downs station.

Some were used for storage and issue of air raid precautionary equipment during the war – their GPO pigeon-holes being ideal for such purposes. No 4954 is recorded as carrying departmental number 1886s between October 1943 and March 1944. Post Office duties resumed after the war but although No 4954 is listed as returning to the Newhaven service, it is not believed that this duty restarted post-1945 so the van became a spare for the London Bridge-Dover runs. It was withdrawn from this service soon after being photographed – in December 1960 – along with fellow sorting vans Nos 4952/53, so it may be inferred that they were still running together as a set. Their replacements were ex-GWR Post Office vans, which in turn were replaced by ex-London Midland vehicles in 1971 – see page 76. *R C Riley, courtesy Rodney Lissenden*

One – Pre-Grouping Passenger Stock

The most numerous ex-London Chatham & Dover Railway coaches on the mainland proved to be the many six-wheel examples built from about 1885 until 1902, with a length of either 28ft or 30ft over body. Examples of these remained in passenger service until December 1936 – latterly on excursions, workmen's and hop-pickers trains. These could vary from seven up to as many as 16 coaches in a set and most would only be seen on high days and holidays when seasonal traffic reached its peak. A few sets were to be occasionally found on the SW section but this stock was most common on South Eastern, and to a slightly more limited extent, on ex-LBSCR lines although the vagaries of excursion traffic might mean they could turn up almost anywhere.

This rather remarkable survivor is a 30ft four-compartment brake third dating from October 1894. Built as LCDR brake second No 48, it became SECR No 2781 in January 1907 (it clearly took a long time to renumber all the ex-Chatham stock after the fusion with the SER in 1899) and then became SR brake third No 3630 on 1 February 1927, to Diagram 173. The guard's side lookouts at this end were also removed and replaced by steel sheeting on this date. It was then formed in SR set No 837 – this being a 14-coach set of LCDR six-wheelers and one of a number formed up by the Southern Railway around that time. Between 1931 and 1934 it was stabled at Crystal Palace and had the following formation: Brake third No 3630, thirds Nos 1633/48, 1761, 1694/07, firsts Nos 7477/61, thirds Nos 1647/93, 1751/19/16, brake third No 3642. By 1935 this had been reduced to 10 coaches by the removal of Nos 1648, 1751, 1719 and 7477 and the set was withdrawn from service during that year. Coach No 3630 was converted into service vehicle No 873s: a mess & tool van allocated to Redbridge sleeper works. It was condemned in October 1949 but reprieved and reallocated to the Outdoor Machinery Department, at Eastleigh, but could still be found at Redbridge.

Withdrawn for the third time in August 1961, it was purchased by the Bluebell Railway, arriving there on 5 February 1962. It is seen at Sheffield Park in May 1962, still in the departmental black livery as purchased but carrying its more recent number DS873. Since acquisition it has been used as a carriage & wagon department store but to date, apart from a 'quick' repaint in green little restoration has been attempted. This was almost certainly the last ex-LCDR six-wheel coach on British Railways, although 10 camping coaches served at various locations until 1954. *R Hobbs*

Turning now to ex-LBSCR stock, this picture lends a new meaning to the term thatched cottage! Grounded at Slindon, West Sussex, probably sometime before the 1920s, this is a former Stroudley 26ft four-wheel brake third from the 1870s. The photograph was taken on 1 October 1976 so it could already have been over 100 years old by then. Its former identity is not known but many of these coaches were built between 1872 and 1892; however, the fact that this coach has no intermediate window partitions marks it out as an early example of a three-compartment brake, probably for suburban block train use.

Several hundred four-wheel vehicles were built – all 26ft long and with many variants amongst the nine basic designs: first, second, third, composite plus brake vehicles of all three classes, etc as well as variations for suburban services (with close couplings, short intermediate buffers and high-density seating) and for main-line use (conventional couplings, long buffers and reduced density seating) and many were later altered or rebuilt as requirements changed.

Some very similar 20ft passenger guards vans were also completed to run with them. Set formations were extremely variable but while some on country branch lines might be as short as three coaches, others in the London suburban area might reach as many as 20 vehicles. The earliest withdrawals came as soon as 1895 but a small number of coaches remained in service to become Southern Railway stock in 1923 – although all except a few transferred to the Isle of Wight were taken out of service during 1924/25, the majority without ever receiving their allocated SR numbers. Several were used in a second-generation Lancing Works train and survived until 1934. Many others were grounded both on and off railway land and a few still survive today – examples of these having been acquired by both the Bluebell and Mid-Hants railways for eventual return to passenger use, mounted on suitably shortened 'utility' van underframes. A visit to the carriage shops at Horsted Keynes at the time of writing will enable similar coaches under restoration to be viewed, giving some idea of the amount of work being undertaken.

This particular example would have been allocated to SR Diagram 169 or 170 – depending on whether it had long buffers at one or both ends; however, all of the 26 brake coaches remaining in 1923 had the usual partitions between compartments, with two quarterlight windows instead of the single large panes. Of these, just the four sent to the Isle of Wight in 1924 and four others transferred to departmental stock ever received any form of Southern livery or numbering. The Island sets each comprised two brake thirds, a third and a composite and ran until October 1931 – set numbers being 495 and 496. *R C Riley, courtesy Rodney Lissenden*

In the sidings at Ryde St Johns on 21 July 1963 is LBSCR 54ft nine-compartment third No S2414 to SR Diagram 90. It may be hard to believe, but the coach began life looking very different to its Isle of Wight appearance. It was built as 6-compartment brake third LBSCR No 638 in the first six months of 1916, becoming SR mainland No 4016, renumbered on 9 December 1924. SR Diagram 203 was allocated and it would have looked very similar to No 4155 on page 33, but would have had side lookouts at the brake end. Formed at one end of three-set No 762, the other coaches were 54ft lavatory composite No 6227 to SR Diagram 347 and 48ft third No 2001 to Diagram 64. The three had previously been LBSCR set No 29, the LBSCR numbers of these two coaches then being 76 and 595 respectively. By 1930 the formation of set No 762 had changed – No 2001 being replaced by another Diagram 203 brake – SR No 4030 – and the set joined the three-coach 'rover' pool, probably by then without lookouts and so was able to run on both Central and South Eastern section services.

In May 1935 both brakes were selected for Isle of Wight transfer but, whereas No 4030 remained as a brake third, No 4016 was rebuilt into a nine-compartment third and renumbered 2414 – one of six such conversions. On arrival the coach was used at first as a loose strengthening vehicle allocated to Newport but was later included in various sets – probably during the summer season only. During the late 1930s and down to 1947 this was usually set No 488 – the other coaches being LBSCR brake thirds Nos 4154/60 and composite No 6356. However, after 1948 formations tended to be less uniform and the coach was noted in sets Nos 497 in 1959, 490 in 1960 and 494 in 1965. These were all six-coach summer formations for the Ventnor line. Withdrawal came in November 1966. *R Hobbs*

Ex-LBSCR 54ft brake thirds came in four-, five-, six- and seven-compartment forms, both on the mainland and on the Isle of Wight. However, whilst the five-compartment versions were easily the most numerous on the mainland, only two ever went to the island. One was lost in a shunting accident at Ryde during World War 2, leaving No 4168 as the last survivor of the genre.

Built in 1922 as LBSCR No 93, it became SR No 3870 on 6 May 1924, along with identical Diagram 198 brake third No 3868 (LBSCR No 87), joining brand new Diagram 337 54ft composite No 6168 (allocated LBSCR No 29 but never applied) in three-coach 'rover' set No 825. This three-set ran until about 1934 when No 3870 was transferred to similar three-set No 819, leaving the other two coaches to run as a two-set for another year or so. In April 1938 No 3870, now without lookouts, was sent to the Isle of Wight, renumbered 4168 and re-allocated to Diagram 230. It was then formed at one end of set No 502, along with Diagram 375 LBSCR composite No 6347 for the Bembridge branch service. The set was usually strengthened by ex-LCDR 42ft seven-compartment third No 2437 during the summer – making an interesting, and possibly unique, combination.

In the 1950s it was often a loose coach based at Newport but, by 1960-63, was at one end of set No 486, with two ex-SECR 54ft 1in rebuilt vehicles. During the last summer of steam it was in set No 500 and was finally used for mail traffic, where the large guard's van proved invaluable. It was photographed at Ryde St Johns on 8 October 1966, while fulfilling this function. Withdrawn in January 1967, the coach was then purchased by the Isle of Wight Steam Railway and is currently operational after extensive repairs to its underframe. This underframe was, incidentally, a reconditioned one that had previously seen service in a World War 1 ambulance train. *R Denison*

One – Pre-Grouping Passenger Stock

Six-compartment LBSCR brake third No 4155 stands in the sidings at Ventnor on 3 September 1965. A total of 15 ex-LBSCR six-compartment brakes, of two types, were shipped to the Isle of Wight. The most numerous were the 10 to SR Diagram 210, arriving in 1936/37: Nos 4151-56/63-66. This coach was built as LBSCR No 650 during 1916; equipped with vacuum slip gear, it would have originally had a third window in the centre of the brake end. This became mainland SR No 4028 on 26 August 1924, being formed in three-set No 821 along with similar slip-fitted seven-compartment brake third No 4039 (ex-LBSCR No 109). The SR Diagrams were originally 203 and 204 respectively.

The centre coach was 54ft lavatory composite No 6230 (LBSCR No 91 – built new in June 1924 so the pre-Grouping number was carried, if at all, for just two months), to Diagram 347. Again part of the three-set 'R' pool until May 1936, both brakes then went to the Isle of Wight, being renumbered 4155 and 4160 respectively. Diagram numbers were now amended to 210 and 211 respectively, to reflect belatedly the fact that the lookouts had been removed. For No 4028/4155, the slip gear was removed in February 1930, although the centre end window remained until sometime after transfer to the island.

As may be seen, the brake end is now fully steel-sheeted, whilst some simplification of the side panelling has also taken place. Once on the Island, the coach was placed at one end of set No 489, with identical brake third No 4156 and ex-LBSCR 48ft thirds Nos 2410/11 and 48ft composites Nos 6362/63 and allocated to Ryde for Ventnor services. After Nationalisation the coach was noted in sets Nos 493, 494 and finally 500, as seen here. Withdrawal is recorded as January 1966. *R Hobbs*

Seven-compartment brake third No 4157 at Ryde St Johns on 10 September 1965 – clearly ex-works. A Diagram 211 vehicle, this went to the Island in May 1936 and was formerly mainland SR No 4035 to Diagram 204. Built in 1912 as LBSCR No 88, it received SR livery and number on 14th January 1927, in SR three-set No 767.

Its companions were then six-compartment brake third No 4021 (LBSCR No 643) to Diagram 203 and lavatory composite No 6226 (LBSCR No 75 and new in late 1923) to Diagram 347. Again from the three-set 'R' pool, both brakes went to the Island in May 1936, where No 4157 was then formed into set No 485, along with composite No 6353 and six-compartment Diagram 210 brake third No 4151, strengthened by Diagram 90 third No 2415 during the summer periods. This formation was retained until 1948 at least, after which the coach 'did the rounds' of sets Nos 500 (in 1950), 487 (1959/60) and 488 (1963-65) at least. Withdrawal came in February 1966 on closure of the Newport/Cowes route – just months after overhaul! *R Hobbs*

A Diagram 373 composite at Ventnor, No 6352 still retains BR crimson lake livery on 31 July 1960. By this date relatively few Island coaches were still in this colour – although the unidentified SECR 54ft 1in Diagram 40 third behind also still is (from a study of other photographs this coach may well be SR No 2447, while identical coach No 2438 in green is on the right – all three were allocated to set No 493 for that year).

Composite No 6352 began life in June 1924 as SR mainland No 6171 to Diagram 337, in three-set 'R' No 824. Its LBSCR number was 70, but this may never have been carried. Its companion brake thirds were SR Nos 3869 and 3871, both being five-compartment coaches to Diagram 198, so would have been similar to No 4168 seen previously on page 32. All three were sent to the Isle of Wight in 1937 – the brakes being rebuilt as full thirds while the composite was re-diagrammed to 373, with one first-class compartment demoted to third class – the third one from this end. At first it was included in mixed origin set No 494 with some ex-LCDR coaches but, for much of its island life, it was a loose coach and appeared in set No 493 in 1959/60 and No 497 between 1962 and 1965.

Withdrawal came in September 1966, by which time all first-class compartments had been reclassified as second. This coach retained most of its timber panelling to the end, yet sister-vehicles Nos 6348/51/53 were almost fully steel-sheeted. *R Denison*

One – Pre-Grouping Passenger Stock

A rare view of an LBSCR pull-push set in malachite green and perhaps not the clearest of images. 'M7' No 30049 and set No 723 are seen at Midhurst on 1 December 1951. This set was formed in late 1922, comprising nine-compartment trailer composite LBSCR No 658 (with two first-class compartments – nearest the locomotive) and six-compartment driving brake third LBSCR No 1410 – the last of six additional units described 'for branch line use' – no specific allocation being stated. Both coaches were the usual 54ft long and had a side corridor and gangways between the two; not that there is anything in the construction to make them look different from any other ex-LBSCR compartment stock.

Prior to Grouping, no set number was allocated; after 1923 the pair became SR set No 990 but, although this was soon applied on the LBSCR umber finish, the two coaches were not renumbered or repainted in SR livery until 7 January 1927. Numbers were then 6250 for the composite (Diagram 351) and 3855 for the brake vehicle (Diagram 194). Originally allocated to Eastbourne for the 'Cuckoo' line and trips along the main line to St Leonards, by 1935 the set had moved to Hastings for the service to Rye. In 1937 it was renumbered as set 723, to clear the number range above 980 for additional electric stock trailer sets, then being numbered downwards from 1000, while in 1939 the set moved to the Seaton branch – probably the only time such a set travelled so far west. It remained there until 1949, returning to the Central section and the Petersfield-Midhurst-Pulborough service.

When photographed it still had the coach numbers in the eaves panels at each end, with an 'S' prefix but without the company title. Shortly after, it was repainted in crimson lake – the livery in which the set ended its days in October 1960, by then with most of the timber panelling covered by steel sheeting. During the mid-1950s it moved to Tonbridge and could be seen on either the Eastern section Westerham and Hawkhurst branches or the Central section lines to Tunbridge Wells West, Oxted or Three Bridges. *G W Powell, courtesy The South Western Circle*

Identical set No 721 at Ash Green on the LSWR Tongham line on 5 October 1957; this was the occasion of the Railway Enthusiasts Club (REC) 'Compass Rose' tour of branch lines around Berkshire, Surrey and Hampshire. Motive power at the rear was an equally spotless 'M7': No 30051. The set is now in crimson lake and is almost completely steel-sheeted. Nearest the camera is Diagram 194 driving brake third No 3853 (ex-LBSCR No 1408), while behind is the Diagram 351 composite No 6248 (ex-LBSCR No 656). Both date from 1922 and, from Grouping until 1937, carried the set number 988; it was changed then to No 721. The coaches were repainted in Southern livery on 9 March 1927.

Although it is not apparent from the picture, we are actually viewing the corridor side of both vehicles. Contributor Mike Rhodes is amongst the group seen, but cannot be identified. The set was originally based at Littlehampton for services to Ford, Bognor Regis, Arundel and probably as far afield as Horsham or Three Bridges, such were the lengths of some main-line pull-push workings before 1938, but after electrification of the mid-Sussex line the set moved around both the Central and South Eastern sections until withdrawn in May 1958. However, it was noted on the NRA special service over the Brookwood-Bisley branch around 1950 – then still almost fully timber-panelled. *R C Riley, courtesy Rodney Lissenden*

One – Pre-Grouping Passenger Stock

One of the former AC stock conversions of 1931, set No 650, is seen near High Brooms on 20 June 1959, propelled by an 'H' class 0-4-4T. One of the ex-SECR 'air control vans' is between the locomotive and the pull-push set and this alone is in Southern Region green livery. The pull-push set is still in unlined crimson lake, with left-hand end numbering – as it had been outshopped around 1949-51 or 1952. The last date that this position was used is not entirely certain, but could be as late as March 1952. Clearly only revarnishing (at best) has taken place in the following seven or eight years.

Details of the coaches were given in *Southern Vans & Coaches in Colour* Plate 79 so will not be repeated here. The head code indicates Tonbridge-Brighton via Eridge but more likely the train will be heading for Oxted or Three Bridges once it leaves Tunbridge Wells West, where the code hopefully will be changed. Coupling of the pull-push locomotive chimney to train was very much more common on the South Eastern section – particularly from Tonbridge – than anywhere else on the Southern. The set had by then just another three months in service, being withdrawn in the following September and broken up at Newhaven before the year was out. *Rodney Lissenden*

Another LBSCR pull-push set in by now rather faded crimson lake with left-hand end numerals; this is set No 716 at Allhallows-on-Sea in the summer of 1960 – not long before withdrawal which occurred on 8 October. This appears to have been its last duty. It had even photographed being hauled by a Crompton diesel on the branch during that year – although not in pull-push mode one hastens to add!

Unlike the sets already illustrated, this has a greater proportion of first-class accommodation with four compartments given over to this class. Both coaches have side corridors and gangways between the coaches, to facilitate issue of tickets by the guard and, again, we are viewing the corridor side but this is not at all obvious. The nine-compartment trailer composite is No 6239, formerly LBSCR No 647 while the eight-compartment driving brake third is SR No 3848, formerly LBSCR No 1403. SR Diagram numbers are 350 and 193 respectively. Both coaches date from late 1921 and would not have been given a set number by the LBSCR. After Grouping they became SR set No 983 and by 1924 this was allocated to Eastbourne for services to Hastings and Rye, but by 1931 it was on the Seaford branch. The two coaches were renumbered on 14 February 1928 – the date on which they were ex-works in Maunsell green livery.

In 1937 the set number was changed to 716, by which time it was allocated to the South Eastern section. It appears to have remained there until withdrawal, either operating from Ashford for the Hythe or New Romney branches, Bexhill West and finally Gravesend for the Allhallows branch. *R Denison*

A delightful period piece – 'H' class tank No 31522 has arrived at Three Bridges from Tunbridge Wells West during the summer of 1959 and the young fireman seems surprised that anyone should want to take a picture of him or his engine! The other staff remain oblivious on the platform. Locomotive and stock are both clean – the set number 714 is just visible on the coach solebar, telling us that we are looking at composite No 6237 (ex-LBSCR No 645 of 1921) and destined to be the last ordinary ex-LBSCR passenger coach on the mainland – withdrawn in July 1961.

The earlier history of this set is similar to No 716 seen in the previous picture, but in December 1944 its companion coach – driving brake third No 3846 (ex-LBSCR No 1401) was taken out of the set and allocated to the Midhurst branch as a loose vehicle. Its place was taken by ex-SECR driving brake third No 3467 to Diagram 166 soon after, which is how the set remained for the rest of its working life. Because this vehicle had no corridor connection, this fitting was also removed from No 6237, resulting in the diagram number being revised from 350 to 350A.

In revised form the set was used on both the South Eastern and latterly on the Central sections, being noted at almost every location on both divisions where pull-push services regularly operated! Most of the former timber mouldings have now been covered by steel sheeting but a few cantrail panels remain. The coach number is clearly now at the right-hand end – the normal arrangement from around 1952 onwards – so placed to be conveniently near the dimension, tare weight and route restriction plates which were mounted low down on the left-hand side of each end. Carriage & wagon department staff might need to consult both in the course of their work and placing the number at the left-hand end involved more walking to see the coach details! No 6237 was finally broken up at Newhaven in October 1962, having spent the time since withdrawal amongst the 140+ coaches stored on the Ardingly branch. *B Blacklock, courtesy R Denison*

One – Pre-Grouping Passenger Stock

The other last surviving ex-LBSCR coach on the mainland was in a very different league altogether. This was the railway's Directors' inspection saloon No 60, dating from 1914, although, because of World War 1, it is believed it did not enter service until 1918. It was, almost certainly, the Brighton's finest piece of carriage construction and very different to the usual low arc-roofed stock.

At 61ft over body and running on six-wheeled bogies, it had a 26ft observation saloon at one end with 18 seats grouped around a long table while, at the other, there was a smaller saloon with six comfortable armchairs around a much smaller table. Later this saloon was re-arranged to provide nine armchairs. Connecting the two saloons was a side corridor giving access to a kitchen, pantry and lavatory. No guard's brake compartment was included, so in pre-Grouping days a 30ft six-wheel passenger brake van, LBSCR No 380, was reserved to run with it. The coach was painted in LBSCR umber, lined in gold and was normally kept at Brighton Works. Once in Southern ownership it was allocated the departmental stock number 291s and Diagram No 1851, in due course receiving Maunsell lined green livery.

At some time between 1934 and 1945 various modifications were made, including the fitting of end gangways and sliding window ventilators in place of the previous top-hung small opening windows – those in the ends were not changed so give an idea of the previous arrangement. This probably did much to relieve the stuffy atmosphere inside the coach on hot days. After 1948 the coach received crimson lake and cream colours and the number DS291. It was now kept at Stewarts Lane. On the day of the photograph – 25 July 1961 – it was on a tour to various Sussex lines behind immaculate 'D1' class 4-4-0 No 31749 and is seen south of Sanderstead station.

The other coach in green is one of the Maunsell restriction 1 unclassed open brake vehicles built originally for South Eastern boat trains in 1933, this providing the guard's accommodation and possibly also seating for 'lesser' staff. In November 1962 the saloon also received green livery and was withdrawn in July 1965. As a vehicle of special interest, it was offered to the BRB Curator of Historic Relics for preservation, but, when this fell through, the coach was purchased by the Bluebell Railway, arriving there on 4 August 1965. There it was occasionally used for Sunday afternoon tea trains until about 1968 or so and some work to restore it to LBSCR umber livery was started. However, it has now been out of service for many years and, although stored under cover, it is estimated that restoration to traffic will cost in excess of £100k. Small wonder it is not high on the priority list. *R Hobbs*

Southern Rolling Stock in Colour

The bleak expanse of Dungeness beach, seen on 6 May 1979. Two former LBSCR six-wheelers are nearest the camera – already partly covered by roofing felt and other domestic extensions. By this date all visible signs of former identity had gone, but when the late Roger Kidner visited the location on 18 September 1930 both coaches still showed many traces of former Southern Railway livery. The passenger brake van on the right was once SR No 733 from set No 909, withdrawn as long ago as January 1929 and subsequently sold off from either Lancing or Ashford Works. This was a 26ft Billinton full brake built originally as LBSCR No 141, in 1894. This was to SR Diagram 898 – one of 32 to be allocated a Southern number – which fell in the range 707-737, along with No 738 being an older Stroudley version of the same type. The last examples were withdrawn from general service in 1932, most previously being formed at each end of a set of other six-wheel coaches, although several lingered awhile in departmental stock.

The other coach is a 32ft five-compartment second (by then third) SR No 1956, withdrawn in September 1929, running latterly in set 966. This was built in 1896 as LBSCR second No 1764, later reduced to third class but keeping the same number. This was one of over 125 such vehicles built between 1895 and 1905. Of these, 52 survived to become all-third class to SR Diagram 63, plus another 49 that became composites to either Diagram 323 or 324 after the Grouping. Most were withdrawn in 1928/29, having been ousted from Central section suburban routes by electrification. Set 909 comprised two six-wheel vans with one or two thirds and two composites between them – one of at least 15 such sets used in country areas (set numbers noted include 884/86/87/94/95, 904-6/9/10/12-14/17/35) while set No 966 was one of at least 23 sets of six-wheelers, usually of six to eight vehicles, used on suburban services. Set numbers noted include 896-903/18/19/38/60-69/72/73.

The house with the 'Birdcage' observatory behind is a former SER four-wheel passenger brake van built between 1872 and 1895 – one of several grounded at Dungeness in the 1920s. *R C Riley, courtesy Rodney Lissenden*

Post-Grouping Passenger Stock

2

Taken from *The Railway Gazette* from late 1927, this print gives some idea of the lining applied to Southern Railway stock of the period – even if the shade of green may be questionable. It is actually a stylised version of an official monochrome view taken in Clapham Yard with the background and foreground edited somewhat.

Combined first-class dining saloon and kitchen car No 7861 was completed in May 1927, to SR Diagram 2651, for main-line services to Bournemouth and Portsmouth. It was originally coupled with eight-bay diner third No 7867 to Diagram 2652 – the coach just seen beyond – one of six pairs completed in that year. At that time there were few other Maunsell coaches available for them to run with and they were usually inserted into ex-LSWR 'Ironclad' sets numbered between 431-435 and 444 – in fact the coach to the left is an 'Ironclad' although this is only apparent in the black & white photograph – and known as six-coach dining sets type A. This general design was repeated with minor alterations for all other Maunsell restaurant cars built until 1934 – a total of 46 coaches in all. Four different diagrams were originally allocated but these only differentiated between the types of cooking range fitted internally.

Externally the only differences concerned the lack of provision of a vestibule end door instead of the plain window at the nearer end in the original six and the details of the window ventilators, which varied from batch to batch. By 1939 the six original cars had received the recessed end door and so were practically identical to all the others. The lining is shown probably as correctly as 1927 block making would allow but was a fine $1/8$in yellow line with a ½in black line and the window frames/droplights picked out in teak; this latter feature often being repainted green in subsequent overhauls.

Note also the roof boards: lettered 'Waterloo Southampton West' and 'Bournemouth' respectively. These again reflect the original photograph. Coach No 7861 became an ambulance car for a period during World War 2 while railway catering services were suspended but returned to traffic in 1945 until withdrawn in May 1961. Unlike the catering vehicles just visible on pages 26 and 43 it was never rebuilt. *SR Official/*Railway Gazette

We now come to a series of very interesting stills taken from the DVD *Steaming through Wessex 2*, published by Kingfisher Productions. The writer is grateful to John Harvey for bringing these to his attention and to Roger Hardingham of Kingfisher for permission to reproduce them. The first sequence show 'Schools' class locomotive No 923 in Maunsell green but with Bulleid lettering, dating the shots to no earlier than February 1939 and hauling a down Folkestone train of Maunsell restriction 4 stock, just south of Polhill Tunnel.

In the left-hand picture we see 1935-design Diagram 2008 flush-panelled Maunsell third No 1877, dating from February 1936 and now finished in unlined Maunsell green livery with stone-coloured rexine interior leading a slightly older Maunsell three-set which is clearly in a lighter colour – probably the new Bulleid malachite but it might be the short-lived 'Dover green' decided upon just prior to Bulleid's arrival on the Southern – perhaps the colour of the spectacle cord in the well-known story of Sir Herbert Walker's executive decision about the future colour for Southern stock. Almost certainly a set from the series Nos 221-232; unfortunately neither the set nor the coach numbers are quite legible. However, what is most interesting is the lettering – instead of the full company title the coaches just have the letters 'SR' along the waistline.

The right-hand picture shows the composite coach as it passes the photographer, again with the lettering style clearly visible. The rest of the lettering – coach numbers and door designations – appear in standard Bulleid style in gold shaded black, but the class designations are in the form first and third, not just plain figures. This style of company lettering has so far been unrecorded and it is unknown just how many coaches carried it. With one further exception (another Diagram 2008 third in unlined olive) the rest of the train is in lined Maunsell olive green. One Pullman car is also included to provide catering facilities. *D Seaton, courtesy Kingfisher Productions*

This is the same set on its return working from Folkestone later in the day, behind olive green-liveried 'King Arthur' class No 805, at the same location just west of Otford village. The lighting conditions now appear different and the coach colour appears bluer – therefore more likely to be malachite than Dover green. The same lettering is visible. The set number may be 229 – if so the coaches are Diagram 2102 brake thirds Nos 2761/62 and Diagram 2301 composite No 5672 – a regular on Kent Coast workings from 1932 until 1962. Note also how the low spring sun has highlighted the cream upper panels of the corridor partition.

Most of the other stock in these sequences are painted lined olive green, although there are one or two in a paler colour with the company title abbreviated just to 'Southern', ie not 'Railway' as well so may be in either malachite or Dover green. Every train included as least one Pullman car. From the available evidence, the latest date for these shots is June 1939 – probably slightly earlier as the trees do not have full leaf cover. *D Seaton, courtesy Kingfisher Productions*

Two – Post-Grouping Passenger Stock

Whilst it is not intended to deal with electric stock, this picture has been included while discussing the subject of liveries. It shows Diagram 2601 '4-BUF' buffet car No 12529, unusually at Ore in 1939 – clearly in unlined malachite green while the rest of the unit (No 3084) remains in Maunsell livery; finished simply with two horizontal waist lines. These may be orange/black instead of the usual yellow/black – but this could be due to the lighting conditions as the presumed yellow lettering on the coach end looks to be similar.

The preserved motor coach No 11201 from '4-COR' unit 3142, when on display at Horsted Keynes, featured two horizontal orange lines and some SR painting specifications mention chrome orange instead of yellow as the lining colour. These '4-BUF' units were intended for Victoria-Bognor services so to find one at this location is noteworthy in itself. The units were under construction when Oliver Bulleid took over from Maunsell. The former redesigned the interiors of the buffet vehicles himself, with the result that the other coaches were completed and already painted before the buffet cars were ready. No doubt to draw attention to the redesign, Bulleid ensured that these coaches alone were finished in his livery! Unit 3084 was ex-works in July 1938 and ran until December 1970.

The buffet car was subsequently acquired for preservation by the NRM and later went to the Nene Valley Railway but regrettably later suffered fire damage and had to be scrapped. *S Perrier*

This most interesting picture was taken at Clapham Junction, probably in 1952 or 1953. It shows a whole range of vehicles in different liveries. On the left is Bulleid Diagram 2017 open third No S1480S, new in November 1950 and presumed to still be in the original crimson lake and cream finish with right-hand end numerals but now with the 'S' suffix letter which was a later addition.

At first a loose coach, this was soon included in Southampton boat set No 350 but appears to be running as a loose vehicle on the day in question. The coach remained in service until August 1965. Next comes Maunsell corridor third No S1200 in the 1948 experimental plum and spilt milk livery. Along with Bulleid sets Nos 299 and 788 (see page 52), three Maunsell vehicles received this livery to allow a complete 12-coach train to be formed – but by 1952 this was seldom maintained and the coaches might turn up on any duty – as seen here. No 1200 was a high-window example of SR Diagram 2001 and was completed in October 1933, running as a loose vehicle for its entire life until withdrawn in December 1961. It carried the experimental livery from May 1948 until early 1954. Note the non-standard position of the numerals – peculiar to all the plum and spilt milk stock; the usual position for left-hand end numbers was to the left of the nearest door. The experimental colours failed to wear well and here they look almost chocolate and cream, although some observers described them as exhibiting considerable ripening of the plum and souring of the milk! *Continued overleaf*

Next in the line is one of the two Maunsell cafeteria car rebuilds; this is either No 7939 or No 7954 to Diagram 2675, rebuilt in August 1952, giving the earliest date for the photograph. These were formerly restaurant cars to Diagram 2651 and were part of a move to diversify BR catering and offer lighter snack-type meals. However, although more conversions were authorised, these two remained the only Maunsell examples. They were used mostly on inter-regional services, including Bournemouth-Wolverhampton and Margate-Birkenhead trains as well as some specials and excursions. Both were equipped with British standard (CA type) gangways instead of the more usual SR Pullman type. Both later received Southern Region green livery and were withdrawn in December 1962.

Finally comes an 'Ironclad' eight-set still in malachite green. From the composition of the set this is likely to be one of either No 439 or No 444, both of which included Maunsell vehicles. The four-compartment brake third is to Diagram 213 (with right-hand corridor when viewed from the brake end) while the Maunsell corridor thirds are a low-window example to Diagram 2001 and then a 1935 flush-sided coach to Diagram 2008. Altogether a very interesting collection of stock but not at all untypical of the period. *R C Riley, courtesy Rodney Lissenden*

A Diagram 2501 Maunsell corridor first in departmental use at Chichester on 20 September 1968 – now numbered 081256 in the internal user series, meaning that it could not travel on the main line without special permission. Such stock would normally be confined to a particular yard only. It remains in traffic green livery with the first-class markings still visible on the doors.

This coach was previously No 7216 and was built in November 1927 by Midland Railway Carriage & Wagon Co of Birmingham – one of few contractor-built Maunsell vehicles. It had low-height windows on the corridor side and was intended for Southampton boat traffic. Later it was included in set No 248 – nominally a four-coach formation for SW section services but regularly made up to either a six-dining set (with restaurant car and open third added) or a six-corridor set (with two corridor thirds added) between about 1936 and 1950. As a six-dining set this was derailed in the Byfleet accident of 27 December 1946 when 'Lord Nelson' class 4-6-0 No 851 left the rails at speed owing to poor track drainage. Thanks to the buck-eye couplings the whole train remained upright and only three passengers were injured.

After June 1951 No 7216 returned to being a loose strengthener until withdrawn in September 1959. In June 1960 the coach entered internal use for the Chief Civil Engineer at Exeter, moving just once more to Chichester about 1963. It was finally withdrawn in June 1969 and broken up on site soon after. *D Wigley*

Opposite top: Ex-SECR 'D1' class 4-4-0 No 31739 leaves Redhill for Tonbridge in June 1961, passing the locomotive shed on the left and the southern abutment of Quarry Tunnel on the right, just behind the smoke. The train consists of Maunsell three-set No 222, formed of Diagram 2102 brake thirds Nos 3752/53 with Diagram 2301 composite No 5665 in the centre. It ran in this form from February 1932 until just after the picture was taken – at first on the South Western section but, after 1948, on South Eastern services, finally ending its days on the Central section – all very cosmopolitan. The only change of formation recorded was, between 1945 and 1947, when the set was strengthened to five vehicles by the addition of Maunsell composite No 5652 and third No 1862; the latter was a flush-sided vehicle so might not have exactly matched the other coaches in the set. Not that this would have bothered the Southern at all! In this form the set was used on services from Waterloo to Bournemouth, Weymouth, Salisbury, Exeter and Plymouth.

After withdrawal the two brake vehicles served for another three months until September 1961 at each end of special traffic eight-set No 268. *R Hobbs*

Opposite bottom: An unidentified 'N' class mogul heads a down inter-regional train bound for the South Coast via Kensington Olympia near Salfords in July 1962. The stock is 1936 three-set No 961, by now strengthened to 10 vehicles and in its final year of service and now on special traffic and inter-regional trains only. This was actually the last Maunsell steam-hauled set, completed in August 1936 for duties to the Kent Coast. It was originally formed of Diagram 2113 brake thirds Nos 4249/50 and Diagram 2308 composite No 5701, remaining thus until the start of the 1962 summer services. In the years prior to World War 2 it would have run regularly with a Pullman car included in the rake. These final Maunsell coaches were some of the best; flush-sided with large picture-type windows on the corridor side.

The summer 1962 formation of this set was as follows: Maunsell Diagram 2113 brake third No 4249; Maunsell Diagram 2008 thirds Nos 1904 and 1908; BR standard Mk 1 open third No S3998; Maunsell Diagram 2308 composite No 5701; Bulleid Diagram 2318 composite No 5874; Maunsell Diagram 2001 thirds Nos 1192, 1274 and 1804; and, Maunsell Diagram 2113 brake third No 4250.

Note that by this date all third class compartments had been redesignated second class. Such seasonal and weekend trains as these would soon fall to the Beeching axe and largely disappeared from the timetables after 1963/64. With the exception of the two Diagram 2008 vehicles, all the other Maunsell coaches failed to survive beyond December 1962. A down semi-fast electric service runs alongside, formed of '2-BIL' units. *R Hobbs*

46

Two – Post-Grouping Passenger Stock

Opposite: The 20 Maunsell pull-push sets became the mainstay of such operation after they were formed between 1959 and 1961; indeed they were the only ex-Southern traditional pull-push vehicles to survive into 1963. At the top we see set No 608 on a Bournemouth West-Wimborne-Ringwood-Brockenhurst service at the isolated station of Holmsley, probably in the spring of 1963 just before the reign of the 'M7' tanks was over. The set featured in Plates 98 and 99 of *Southern Vans & Coaches in Colour* so details will not be repeated here, but the air control van is one of the five replacements for the ex-SECR Diagram 960 vehicles: plywood-bodied SR Nos 1621-25 to Diagram 3103, converted to pull-push operation briefly from late 1962 until 1964. In fact, they saw just a few months of pull-push operation as the last 'M7s' were withdrawn in May 1963.

In the lower picture we see set No 609 at Hawkhurst on 20 May 1961, with 'H' class tank No 31543 at the rear. Another location known for its remoteness to the centre of the town it purported to serve, this line closed just three weeks later. This set comprised Diagram 2407 driving brake composite No 6694 and Diagram 2023 trailer open second No 1353, running for just five years from November 1959 until November 1964 – one of the final six survivors – albeit by then not operating in pull-push mode. Like sets Nos 608 and 610, this also found itself part of Western Region assets in January 1963 but was returned to the Southern Region by July 1964, being noted in Salisbury east carriage sidings at that date. The original allocations for the 20 Maunsell pull-push sets were Nos 600-7/16-19 Central section, Nos 608/9/12-15 South Western section and Nos 610/11 to the South Eastern section but clearly, as the picture demonstrates, this very soon changed. *NB Collection/R C Riley, courtesy Rodney Lissenden*

A view of Eridge station in October 1961. A train from Eastbourne to Tunbridge Wells West is in the loop platform, awaiting the connecting service towards Oxted and London, which is already signalled from the up main platform. A BR Standard Class 4 2-6-4T heads Maunsell restriction 1 set No 451 – normally a four-coach formation but running for much of 1961 with a van C in place of one brake third. One of the earlier restriction 1 four-sets with low-height corridor side windows, this dates from February 1929 and was formed of Diagram 2104 brake thirds Nos 4071/72 and Diagram 2302 composites Nos 5163/64. This formation was maintained until the set was split in half early in 1962, apart that is for the period in 1961 where the van C was substituted. After that time set No 451 comprised just Nos 4071 and 5164 only, the other two becoming set No 463. All four coaches were withdrawn in May/June 1964. *R Hobbs*

A commendably clean Tonbridge allocated mogul, No 31411, arrives at the attractive station of Nutfield with a Redhill-Tonbridge train in June 1963. The youthful fireman is clearly keen to be recorded on film – this being one of only eight left-hand drive 'N' class locomotives. The train comprises 'half-set type E' No 446 followed by a pair of utility vans – van 'Cs' in SR parlance, van 'BY' under British Railways. As noted in the caption to the frontispiece, this is clearly an occasion when only one two-set was available for the duty.

The coaches are high-window restriction 1 Maunsells No 3699 (Diagram 2104 brake third) and No 5609 (Diagram 2302 composite) – both ex-four-set No 188 in 1962 and date from February 1931. The other two coaches (Nos 3698 and 5608) remained paired as set No 188. All four were withdrawn in March 1965. Note the recently re-laid flat-bottom rails at this point, the barley-twist gas lamp standards, warning notices, rail-built signal, telegraph poles and all the accoutrements of the trackside of those days – now all vanished. *R Hobbs*

Opposite: A few of the Diagram 2654 unclassed open brake coaches built originally for South Eastern boat trains in 1933 eventually found themselves included in some of the half-sets type E during 1962-65, providing some second-class passengers with an unaccustomed level of comfort.

This is No 4447 at a rather cold Heathfield station on 24 March 1964, formed in two-set No 450 along with composite No 5630, just seen to the left. Set No 450 was originally identical to No 451 seen on page 47; it comprised brake thirds Nos 4069/70 and composites Nos 5161/62, running from January 1929 until January 1962. A new set No 450 was then formed with unclassed open brakes Nos 4447/48 and composites Nos 5630/32, running as a four-set for less than a year before being split in half – the other two coaches being renumbered as set No 461. The pair photographed managed to last until March 1965. Another half-set type E is visible to the right.

The 'Cuckoo' line through Heathfield to Eastbourne was one of their regular duties as some of the trains ran through to Tonbridge, involving passage of the narrow tunnels either side of Tunbridge Wells Central, necessitating the retention of 8ft

Two – Post-Grouping Passenger Stock

6in wide restriction 1 stock until mid-1965 – long after many of them had passed the 'over 30-year age to withdrawal' ruling. The final two were sets Nos 190/92, withdrawn in July 1965, just after closure of the Heathfield line. *M W F Gill*

Some eight-compartment restriction 1 corridor thirds were built – either as loose strengthening vehicles or for inclusion in eight-coach sets. This is internal user No 081315, which served as a goods office at Streatham Common yard and later for National Carriers Ltd between December 1961 and withdrawal in 1973. It was photographed just prior to purchase by the Bluebell Railway on 18 September 1973. It carries a rather faded olive green livery. Built originally in February 1931 as Diagram 2003 third No 2356, it ran in eight-set No 217 between London and Eastbourne. On electrification of this route, the set moved to Kent Coast lines until 1959, when it was reduced to four coaches only. No 2356 became a loose vehicle until withdrawn in June 1961.

After purchase by the Bluebell Railway, the coach received cosmetic external restoration and was used for a time as a carriage & wagon material store at Horsted Keynes. It is currently out of use and awaiting further restoration. *D Wigley*

A rather colourful relief staff breakdown train riding van, No DS70121 is seen at Chart Leacon depot, Ashford, on 19 August 1978. A former restriction 0 Hastings line composite, No 5595 to SR Diagram 2304, this dates from September 1929 and was originally the centre coach of three-set type F No 478, along with Diagram 2105 brake thirds Nos 3678/79. However, it was not long before the amount of first-class accommodation proved insufficient and No 5595 was replaced in the set by all-first No 7403 – this change taking place by early 1931. The displaced composite then became a loose vehicle on Hastings line trains – usually coupled to one of the six restriction 0 Pullman cars and a loose third in the centre of the train between two three-sets until 1958, when it was formed into additional South Eastern section long nine-set No 937 for excursion and special traffic and based at Maze Hill. This only lasted for a year until withdrawal in July 1959. The coach was then stored at various locations until converted into a breakdown van for Tonbridge shed in April 1963, moving on subsequently to Ashford.

By 1980 it had been repainted bright yellow and moved to Selhurst, later Wimbledon. It might still be in use today. *D Wigley*

The first Bulleid coaches were 59ft long – the same length as the previous Maunsell stock – and exhibited many of the same general design features, in particular the individual doors to each compartment, but they adopted the new Bulleid profile. A total of 22 such sets were completed in 1945/46 – many using underframes built around 1940 but stored owing to shortage of the materials needed to complete the bodywork. The final four of these sets were to the new 64ft 6in standard length but still retained individual compartment doors. Diagram 2121 59ft brake third No 2867 dates from January 1946 and was formed in three-set No 976 along with companion brake No 2868 and Diagram 2316 composite No 5722 from March of that year.

It is seen from the compartment side at Clapham Junction on 19 May 1965 – by now running as an eight-set with five additional 64ft 6in later Bulleid vehicles included. It was allocated to the South Western section until September 1961, moving to the Oxted line until 1963 but retaining its original three-coach formation.

By June 1963 the set had been augmented to six vehicles for inter-regional services, increased to eight by 1964 and returned to SW section lines. By the following year the vehicle was running as a loose coach, which is how it remained until withdrawal in July 1967. The lack of additional beading strips to cover failed construction joints probably indicates that this coach has been completely resheeted – it certainly still looks smart. *M W F Gill*

Two – Post-Grouping Passenger Stock

Only one of the 59ft coaches enjoyed a brief afterlife: Diagram 2121 brake third No 2850 from set No 967, which was sold to the Chipman Weed Killing Co of Horsham after withdrawal in November 1965, becoming No CWT13 in its fleet. It is seen from the corridor side while in store at Horsham on 26 March 1977 in rather faded Chipman red and white livery. It had been out of use for some time prior to being photographed and was sold to the Mid-Hants Railway in 1978. There its career also failed to develop and the coach was dismantled to provide spares between 1988 and 1991.

It was built in December 1945, running with companion brake third No 2849 and composite No 5713 on the South Western section until 1959, then on the former Somerset & Dorset joint line until composite No 5713 was withdrawn in December 1963. The set was then augmented to eight vehicles during 1964/65 using later Bulleid stock. *D Wigley*

One of the four 64ft 6in 'multi-door' composite coaches to Diagram 2317 is seen from the corridor side at Clapham Junction on 18 September 1965. The compartment side featured in *Southern Vans & Coaches in Colour* Plate 111 and this shows how different these early Bulleid vehicles looked from both sides. Later Bulleid coaches looked very alike whichever side was viewed. By now the coach has been downgraded to all-second class and renumbered from 5729 to 1729. In this form it ran from August 1964 until withdrawn in September 1967 – at first in three-set No 983 augmented to eight coaches, then, from June 1964, in similarly augmented set No 980 until late 1965, finally as a loose vehicle. *M W F Gill*

In May 1948 several sets of coaches throughout BR were repainted experimentally in either ex-GWR chocolate and cream or ex-LNWR plum and spilt milk livery to test public reaction. Just whether much serious public consultation on these actually took place is arguable, as neither livery was subsequently adopted as standard.

On the Southern, a complete train of Maunsell stock in GWR livery ran on the South Eastern section while on the South Western section Bulleid three-set No 788 and six-set No 299, plus three loose Maunsell coaches (see page 43) received the former LNWR livery; they are seen here leaving Eastleigh behind apple green 'Lord Nelson' class No 30856. Bulleid 3-coach set No 299 is leading the train. The stock originally ran on the 7.20am Bournemouth West-Waterloo and 3.30pm down (1.30pm on Saturdays) return working but in 1949 this was changed to the 9.30am down and 2.20pm up service from Bournemouth. However, the three-set and some of the loose Maunsells certainly served Weymouth and the stock was also seen at Exeter on occasions. Neither the apple green locomotives nor the carriage liveries fared well and No 30856 was repainted in standard BR dark green in early 1950, so this view must date from either 1948 or 1949 – probably the latter as from the shadows the picture appears to be the 9.30am down working leaving Eastleigh in mid-morning. The carriages received crimson lake and cream colours early in 1954 – by which time the original appearance was rather less attractive than seen here. *Photographer unknown*

Opposite: The last original 'Merchant Navy' on the SW section, No 35006 Peninsula & Oriental SN Co takes the 11.54am Waterloo-Salisbury train through Weybridge in the summer of 1959 – just prior to going into Eastleigh Works for rebuilding. The stock is an unidentified Bulleid five-set from the series 830-849, still with left-hand numbering and correctly formed with the composite in the centre, flanked on each side by a corridor third and a semi-open brake third. It was not at all uncommon to find both thirds coupled adjacent to each other – especially in sets Nos 830-837, which were regularly reduced to three coaches during the winter period only. *F Foote*

Two – Post-Grouping Passenger Stock

Southern Rolling Stock in Colour

Many Maunsell coaches entered departmental stock but very few Bulleids were used in this manner. One long-serving example was internal user No 082232, seen above wearing olive green livery at East Croydon on 1 October 1973. This was formerly Diagram 2123 brake third No 2526 from set No 862 and one of the last Bulleid loco-hauled coaches to be completed in June 1951. Its companions in set No 862 were Diagram 2318 composite No 5920 (actually built in February 1950 but stored until the brake thirds were ready) and identical brake third No 2525. This ran as a three-set type L on the SW section from 1951 until 1963, moving to the Central section for a time between then and 1965.

Once set formations were abandoned the coaches returned to the South Western section until withdrawn during 1967. These sets had their intermediate buffers removed around 1960, which probably explains why they retained their formations throughout, but these had to be restored from 1964 onwards as withdrawals started. Coach No 2526 was withdrawn in March 1967, becoming internal user No 082232 – the second coach to carry this number – being used as an office for the Shipping and Continental staff at Newhaven until late 1973 – so when seen at East Croydon was probably on its way to Stewarts Lane for further conversion. This resulted in the coach returning to ordinary departmental stock as No DB975375 – an instruction coach for the Mechanical & Electrical Engineers, Rolling Stock Section – in which form it is seen above left, now painted in rail blue livery at Salisbury on 30 June 1992. It continued to fulfil this function until withdrawn in 1996, when it was sold to VSOE and stored at Eastleigh and later Stewarts Lane. Purchased by the Bluebell Railway in 1999, it has since been fully and magnificently restored to BR Southern Region green livery and is currently in service.

It is believed that, by the 1990s, only one other Bulleid coach remained in BR departmental stock – this being similar vehicle No 4008/internal user No 083641; although this was also purchased by the Bluebell Railway, it was subsequently broken up for spares. *D Gould/M W F Gill*

The final Bulleid set was No 865; this also entered service in June 1951. It is seen leaving Dorking North in June 1963 behind Bulleid pacific No 34057 *Biggin Hill* on the 5.13am London Bridge-Brighton via Steyning newspaper train – one of few steam-hauled services through Dorking North. At the rear are an ex-GWR siphon G and a utility van. The train is about to pass beneath the former SER Redhill-Guildford line bridge.

Set No 865 comprised Diagram 2123 brake thirds Nos 2531/32 with Diagram 2318 composite No 5923 – the latter having been stored since completion a year earlier. Like set No 862, this was originally allocated to the SW section but moved to the Central section between 1963 and 1965. Coach No 2532 was withdrawn in April 1964 and its place taken by similar coach No 4352 for the final year or so – this being one of the former Bournemouth line vehicles with extended side panels – making this set easily recognisable from a distance. The set was deleted from carriage working notices at the end of 1965 and only replacement coach No 4352 would see a further 10 months of service. *R Hobbs*

A broadside view of Diagram 2318 composite No 5902 at Clapham Junction in late 1966 with the shape of things to come behind: a '4-REP' unit in rail blue livery. Built in December 1949 and outshopped in crimson lake and cream with left-hand end numbers (without 'S' suffix) this was a loose coach for its entire existence, being withdrawn in August 1967 along with many of its brethren following the inauguration of full electric services to Bournemouth. At that time most Bulleid coaches were hardly life-expired (all were less than 22 years old) but concerns had been voiced over their impact resistance in a collision if marshalled between all-steel British Railways Mk 1 stock. In addition, the designed load-bearing strength of a Bulleid coach underframe was a mere 80 tons; this was clearly considered sufficient in the 1940s but the equivalent figure for BR coaches was 200 tons. As BR was then finding itself with an excess of coaching stock, it was not difficult to consign the ex-Southern vehicles rapidly to the scrapyards. The May 1967 carriage working notices listed 326 coaches to go for scrap and just 37 to be kept until March 1968. Only 18 of these survived into the latter half of that year on the Southern Region, whilst some were transferred elsewhere; however, none of these remained in passenger traffic beyond 1970. *M W F Gill*

One of the coaches to survive slightly longer was E1474S, seen in lined maroon livery at Cambridge on 10 December 1966. This was one of 20 Diagram 2017 open thirds (now second class) transferred to the Eastern and Scottish regions in 1965 – not because those regions necessarily wanted any Bulleid stock but to balance the loss of Mk 1 coaches taken by the Southern Region for rebuilding into '4-REP' and 'TC' vehicles in advance of the Bournemouth electrification. Eleven went to the Scottish Region, nine to the Eastern Region between September 1965 and February 1966, where some remained in use until, at the latest, February 1970, outlasting similar coaches on the Southern Region by up to two years. No 1474 dates from October 1950 and was always a loose vehicle, going to the ER in September 1965, remaining in service on ex-Great Eastern lines until February 1968. *M Rhodes*

On the final weekend of steam services between Waterloo and Exeter, Saturday 5 September 1964, 'West Country' pacific No 34099 *Lynmouth* leaves Honiton Tunnel with an up stopping train to Yeovil Junction made up unusually of a Bulleid brake composite in lined maroon livery and an LNER Thompson corridor coach. Interestingly, these same two coaches were seen working on the North Cornwall line a fortnight earlier. The Bulleid vehicle is one of the loose worked Diagram 2406 coaches built originally in June-September 1948 for through services between West Country branches and Waterloo, from the number series 6713-52. Of these, Nos 6714-17/19/26/38 were inherited by the Western Region in the boundary changes of January 1963, while Nos 6742/46 were sent there as late as November 1964. Of these, Nos 6716/19 are known to have been repainted in maroon at Swindon Works early in 1964, so the coach pictured is likely to be one of these – in the form No W6716S. All these WR-allocated coaches were withdrawn between November 1964 and February 1966. *R Hobbs*

One of the Bulleid dining firsts to Diagram 2507, No 7677, is seen near Basingstoke on 17 August 1966, while still formed in the remnants of Bournemouth line 6-dining set No 294. The coach began life in similar set No 290 in August 1947 but moved on to set No 294 in 1965. To the right is a BR buffet car, complete with red catering stripe and Commonwealth bogies, while a Diagram 2318 composite is just seen to the left. A catering re-organisation took place in 1962; this steadily removed most of the Bulleid restaurant cars from the Bournemouth line six-sets, replacing them with newer BR Mk 1 buffets, allowing the older coaches to be cascaded onto lesser services. However, this replacement did not extend to the dining saloons, some of which remained on front-line Bournemouth services for a few years longer; in the case of coach No 7677 until as late as September 1967 and the end of the summer timetable. The now unclassed open dining section is nearest the camera, with plenty of roof ventilation while the three first-class compartments served by a side corridor (unseen on the far side in the picture) are at the far end. *M W F Gill*

From 1951 British Railways standard Mk 1 coaches began to appear on the Southern Region, being used turn and turnabout with Bulleid and Maunsell stock. The most numerous type of coach was the four-compartment brake third to BR Diagram 182 and eventually some 192 vehicles received 'S' prefixed numbers and green livery – although most were delivered in 'blood & custard'. By late 1966 electric services had reached Basingstoke and Southampton, allowing some Mk 1 stock to be released back to other regions. No M34256 was one, seen at Bournemouth Central in either late 1966 or 1967 (the centre roads have already been removed) but still retaining green livery and, by the look of it, still on a Waterloo service. This coach dates from mid-1952 and was originally formed at one end of four-set No 877, along with companion brake third No S34255, composite No S15035 and corridor third No S24313, allocated to South Western section services. Apart from a short period in 1959 when the set was augmented to 10 coaches using Bulleid stock, this formation was maintained until 1962, when the third (now second) was removed from the set. As a three-coach formation, the vehicles continued to run until early 1966, when set formations were disbanded. Presumably the coach did find its way to the LM Region and a repaint in blue and grey – it was transferred there officially from December 1966 but had been withdrawn by 1974. *A King*

Southern Rolling Stock in Colour

A glorious summer's day on the Hayling branch – Saturday 27 July 1963 – and 'A1X' No 32670 has just left Havant with a packed train of daytrippers heading for the island. The train is formed of a BR standard Mk 1 non-corridor second and Maunsell pull-push set No 619 – although, by this time, the two coaches were listed as working separately and certainly not in pull-push mode. On this day they just happen to be coupled together. Coach numbers are 1331 for the Diagram 2023 open second, 6699 for the Diagram 2407 brake composite at the rear of the train. Whilst the brake vehicle was withdrawn soon after closure of the Hayling Island line, the open coach continued to run as a loose pull-push relief vehicle until November 1964 – the same date as the last six surviving Maunsell pull-push sets were withdrawn. The BR coach is likely to be one of Nos S46284/91-93 to BR Diagram 327, some of which were allocated to the line from 1958 until closure. The June 1963 carriage working notice appendix lists the two sets as follows: Nos S46284, 6697, S46291; and, Nos S46292, 6699, S46293. There was no mention of second No 1331; however, the fibreglass coach No S1000S was allocated to the line soon after so it seems that the operators had more vehicles available to them than officially listed. *R Hobbs*

Two – Post-Grouping Passenger Stock

A cold and frosty morning at Kensington Olympia station in October 1962 with 'H' class No 31305 and the empty stock of the Post Office workers' train about to return to Clapham Junction. This is set No 156 – the regular on this duty from May 1959 until its demise in July 1967 – although the actual formation varied considerably over the years. It began as four SECR 'long tens' and a Maunsell brake third in various incarnations as centre vehicle but, from June 1962, was as seen here, with BR Mk 1 non-corridor seconds Nos S46284/90/94 and Maunsell Diagram 2113 Brake No 4245 – the second vehicle from the engine. This was one of the final 1936 Maunsell vehicles with large corridor side windows – clearly visible in this picture – and remained in the set until withdrawn in December 1963 – its place then being taken by a Bulleid vehicle. By the following year coach No 46284 had moved to Hayling and been replaced on the 'Kenny Belle' by sister-vehicle No 46289 while, later still, the fibreglass coach No S1000S also appeared in the set. *R Hobbs*

3 Pullman Cars

This picture could have been placed as the final one in section two, as it includes both a BR standard vehicle and a Pullman car. The up 'Bournemouth Belle' passes Vauxhall on Friday 7 July 1967 – the final weekday of steam operation, while the 'Belle' also had just two more days to run. Motive power is Brush Type 4 (now Class 47) No D1922, while the first coach is a BR Diagram 711 full brake in green – one of just 18 such vehicles transferred to the Southern from the LMR in November 1965 – and probably some of the last Mk 1 loco-hauled coaches to receive green livery. This is No S81510 but the rest were Nos S80561/94/695/875/93/926/33/45/49, 81039/50/153/273/89/92/345/542. All remained allocated to the Southern and eventually received either blue and grey or all-blue livery. In fact, by the date of the photograph, at least two had already been repainted blue and grey and could also be seen as the front and rear coaches on the Bournemouth Belle. In the early 1960s the Southern had managed to appropriate (pinch!) two chocolate and cream Western Region allocated vans (Nos W80713/14) for the train. These matched the Pullman car livery well.

Pullman No 75 was a second class (ex-third class) 'K' type parlour car dating from 1928 – one of 24 all-steel cars built by Metropolitan for services on the LNER. It was to Pullman Diagram 95P, seating 42 passengers in seven bays of six and was 63ft 10in long over vestibules and 8ft 7in wide, running on 10ft wheelbase pressed steel bogies. During World War 2 it was taken into LNER stock as its No 481, receiving all-over brown livery and probably did not arrive on the Southern Region until about 1961, when the 12-wheeled wooden-bodied cars on the 'Bournemouth Belle' were replaced by more modern vehicles. It was probably withdrawn a few days after being photographed and sent to Oatlands sidings at Walton-on-Thames to await scrapping. However, this was not the end for car No 75 as it was purchased by Ind Coope Ltd and installed at The Spot Gate Inn, Hilderstone, Staffordshire, being incorporated into a restaurant adjoining the public house, along with parlour first *Ursula*. Both cars remain there to this day. *R C Riley, courtesy Rodney Lissenden*

Three – Pullman Cars

A rather older 12-wheeled car, first-class buffet *Grosvenor* at Eardley Road sidings on 18 April 1960 – not long before withdrawal. This car had a most interesting and varied history and was, at the time, the oldest Pullman still in ordinary service. Built in November 1908 for the LBSCR's 'Southern Belle', it was one of seven completed by the Metropolitan Amalgamated Railway Carriage & Wagon Co at its works in Lancaster. Each was magnificently finished and constructed to the limit of the Brighton's generous loading gauge, measuring 63ft 10in long over vestibules, 8ft 8¾in wide and no less than 13ft 6in high overall, and running on 12ft wheelbase six-wheel bogies. Note the full-width entrance vestibules – unlike most later Pullman cars. *Grosvenor* was a buffet car and included a small pantry, a buffet counter, with seats for 25 passengers in three sections and a ladies' lavatory at the end farthest from the buffet area. Publicity of the era was most gushing about the interior of the cars but undoubtedly no expense had been spared to guarantee passenger comfort. Electrification of the Brighton main line in 1933 caused most of the former 'Southern Belle' cars to be withdrawn by 1935 but *Grosvenor* was reprieved because, by then, it had been fitted with a new kitchen complete with Fletcher Jennings cooking range and so was worth keeping. In 1936 it was extensively rebuilt, including being reduced in height by one foot to enable the car to run on South Eastern and South Western section lines. It now had a kitchen, pantry, long bar counter with 11 stool-type seats and eight further unclassed loose armchairs with tables at one end. The Pullman Car Co Diagram was then 12K and it was classed as a Pullman Type S. Similar car *Myrtle* (built in 1911) was dealt with in a like manner. We are here viewing the corridor or non-bar side – the other side looked very different with only two large and two smaller frosted windows (in the kitchen area) near each end. It was later used on Southampton boat trains, the 'Golden Arrow' and finally on the Victoria-Newhaven Harbour service (along with car Myrtle) until withdrawn in October 1960. It was then sold to BR Eastern Region for £878 and converted into their camping coach No CC169, repainted light blue and located, most probably, at a coastal station in either Norfolk or Suffolk. Final withdrawal took place in 1968. *R C Riley, courtesy Rodney Lissenden*

Twelve-wheel car *Hibernia* at Eardley Road sidings on 30 October 1960. This was a first-class kitchen 'H' type car, built for LBSCR service by Cravens of Sheffield in January 1914, measuring 63ft 6in over vestibules, 8ft 7in wide but only 12ft 7in high. During World War 1 the car was allocated to the War Office for special duties, so may have been used by King George V, the Prime Minister and other top officials when travelling to Folkestone or Dover on visits to the Western front. After the war the car returned to LBSCR services, running in the 'Southern Belle' and to Eastbourne, Brighton, Portsmouth and other destinations in trains formed otherwise of ex-LBSCR non-corridor stock. In 1925 it was equipped with a small pantry and in May 1933 the car was remodelled at Preston Park workshops into a composite (there were never very many of these), now with a kitchen, larger pantry, 16 third-class and 12 first-class seats, to Pullman Car Co Diagram 23K. During World War 2 it was noted stored in Sidley goods yard (on the Bexhill West branch) and was remodelled to first class prior to return to service in July 1947, now with 20 seats. In 1950 the former timber mouldings and vertical match boarding was covered by aluminium sheeting – making the car look rather more modern – and it continued in use on SW and SE section boat trains and the 'Bournemouth Belle'. Withdrawn by the date of the picture, it was sold to BR Southern Region for £1,276 and converted into camping coach No P46 ready for the 1961 season, located firstly at Hinton Admiral and later at Lyndhurst Road. It was scrapped in 1968. Beyond may be seen kitchen car *Rosalind*, built in 1921 and destined to become SR Pullman camping coach No P47. *R C Riley, courtesy Rodney Lissenden*

Three – Pullman Cars

Pullman camping coach No SC41 at Morar, on the line to Mallaig and finished in pale blue livery, on 2 July 1962. This was formerly parlour first *Sunbeam*, completed in June 1921 by the Pullman Car Co at its Longhedge (Battersea) works – one of 12 built in 1920/21 for the SECR: six parlour and six kitchen cars. They would have originally run in pairs and would have carried lake livery when delivered, to match the colours of other SECR stock. If run as a complete train of Pullmans, the first and last coach were usually one of the SECR's 'birdcage' corridor brake composite vehicles as at that time few Pullman brake cars were available. At first a Type B car, this was revised to Type H *circa* 1932; its dimensions were the same as *Hibernia* in the previous picture. Originally the car seated 27 first-class passengers, with a gentleman's lavatory at one end, a small pantry at the other. Diagram 28P was allocated, but the seating was later reduced to 26 persons. Once on Southern Railway services the cars would have been repainted umber and cream and would have provided catering facilities on South Eastern section expresses and boat trains, running with ex-SECR 'Continental', Maunsell stock and later with Bulleid vehicles. After World War 2 some would also have been seen on SW section boat trains and the 'Bournemouth Belle'. *Sunbeam* was plated over in 1952 and withdrawn in October 1960, becoming Scottish Region camping coach No SC41 in time for the 1961 season – one of 11 eventually sent there. These proved to be the final camping coaches on BR and were withdrawn in 1969 or 1970. *M Rhodes*

Eight-wheeled 'G' class Pullman car *Savona* at Eardley Road sidings on 18 April 1960. This was originally a parlour car built by Birmingham RCW Co in 1910 – one of 12 new vehicles for SECR services. Somewhat smaller in dimensions than those so far illustrated, it was 57ft 6in long over vestibules and 8ft 6in wide. Again painted lake in pre-Grouping days, it was remodelled to a kitchen car in January 1924, now with 16 first-class seats, to Pullman Car Co Diagram 64K. It was probably repainted umber and cream at the same time. A further remodelling took place in 1937, when an individual compartment seating four was removed, although the total number of seats remained at 16. Diagram 103K was then allocated. Here we are looking at the corridor side of the coach – with the kitchen area on the far side, behind the right-hand pair of windows with a handrail across them. Cars *Emerald*, *Palermo*, *Sapphire* and *Sorrento* were similar. During World War 2 the car was noted parked in Tonbridge goods yard, returning to work after the war on South Eastern section boat trains. At some point in the late 1950s the original equalising beam bogies were replaced by standard SR 8ft wheelbase ones – taken from '2-NOL' electric vehicles – and the car was withdrawn in December 1960, becoming Scottish Region camping coach No SC44 at Corpach in the following year. *R C Riley, courtesy Rodney Lissenden*

Three – Pullman Cars

We now come to the 'K' class cars running on 10ft wheelbase plate-frame bogies – the most standardised group of Pullman cars built from 1923 to 1928. They were all 63ft 10in long over vestibules and, apart from the six narrow Hastings line cars, either 8ft 6in or 8ft 7in wide. All had wooden bodies and separate underframes with heavy steel angle trussing – unlike the post 1928 all-steel cars that did not feature truss rods. This is *Sappho*, built by the Midland Railway Carriage & Wagon Co in November 1924; this was a 22-seat kitchen car based mostly on the South Eastern section. Pullman Car Co Diagram 73K was allocated – one of six to this diagram. The *Railway Gazette* for late 1924 described these cars, stating that they were primarily for the 10.50am Victoria-Dover boat train and 5.30pm return working, noting that they were painted umber and cream instead of lake livery, while the internal finish of *Sappho* included mahogany panelling with satinwood inlays, a blue trellis-pattern carpet and biscuit coloured moquette coverings on the chairs, finished with a blue trellis pattern. All six cars featured different interior finishes. Noted on the 'Devon Belle', 'Golden Arrow' and 'Bournemouth Belle' in the 1950s and 1960s, by about 1957 all exterior wooden mouldings were covered by aluminium sheeting and the car was finally withdrawn in September 1963. Here we are looking at the kitchen side – occupied by the section with the frosted glass window – while the adjacent small pantry is lit by the oval 'cathedral' window. Note the one remaining roof board – labelled 'The Cunarder' indicating final employment on Southampton boat expresses. The picture was taken at Eardley Road sidings on 28 March 1963. *R C Riley, courtesy Rodney Lissenden*

Also at Eardley Road on 28 March 1963 was Diagram 87K buffet car *Cecilia* – one of six to this diagram as well. Structurally almost identical to *Sappho*, this was again built by Midland Railway Carriage & Wagon Co of Birmingham, but built four years later in November 1927. This again seated 22 passengers but in a slightly different configuration. Apart from external resheeting to cover the timber mouldings and lower side match boarding, *circa* 1955, this car was not altered during its working life – unusual for a Pullman car as most received several remodelling's during their careers to keep abreast of changes in public taste. Withdrawal came in December 1963. *R C Riley, courtesy Rodney Lissenden*

Three – Pullman Cars

At Old Oak Common on 12 September 1964 is 'K' class car *Penelope* – on loan from the Southern Region for the 'South Wales Pullman' relief set – although it may not have actually seen any use on the train. This was built by Metropolitan Carriage, Wagon & Finance Co in 1927 and was to Diagram 83K – one of five to this diagram. These seated only 20 first-class passengers and had a larger kitchen than the cars in the previous two pictures. We are looking here at the corridor side – the kitchen being on the far side at the right-hand end. Despite the date, the car still exhibits the older Pullman coat of arms, superseded in 1959. Originally with timber mouldings and match boarding, it was sheeted over some time in the 1950s. This car was originally allocated to SW section ocean liner expresses while, in the later 1930s, it was used on the Imperial Airways' Empire Service. After World War 2 the car was briefly reduced to third class as No 150 – serving on the LNER in this form in 1950 – but was soon returned to first class and the 'Devon Belle', moving back to the Eastern Region for the 'Master Cutler' and 'Yorkshire Pullman' before returning to the Southern Region about 1963. It was withdrawn in August 1966. *R C Riley, courtesy Rodney Lissenden*

The final Pullman picture shows 'K' class car *Diamond* at Eardley Road on 28 March 1963 – and a master of many disguises! Built by Birmingham RCW Co in late 1924 or early 1925, it was originally a parlour car named *Octavia* and was sent to Italy. Returned in 1928, by which time this name had been reused here, it was overhauled by BRCW, provided with a kitchen and renamed *Diamond*, entering service on the 'Golden Arrow' and having the usual 22 first-class seats similar to cars *Sappho* and *Cecilia*. In April 1946 it was remodelled as a buffet car, with just 12 seats and a large cocktail bar, to Pullman Car Co Diagram 4K. It would have probably retained the name *Diamond* had it not been for the fact that the 'new' Trianon Bar car (a rebuild of a much older vehicle) ran hot on the inaugural run of the post-war 'Golden Arrow' on 13 April 1946. *Diamond* was hastily got ready as substitute on 15 April and renamed *Trianon Bar*, but once the original car had been repaired, *Diamond/Trianon* was renamed *The One Hundred Bar* to celebrate the centenary of the Dover-Ostend boat service in July 1946; it was then renamed *The New Century Bar* a few weeks later, once the 100th anniversary had passed! Both names appeared on the bar (ie other) side in Gothic lettering in the form of a scroll. By 1950 the car was on the Channel Islands/St Malo service between Waterloo and Southampton Docks. In May 1955 it moved to the Western Region and was renamed again – this time as *Diamond: Daffodil Bar* – for the 'South Wales Pullman' service. It was probably aluminium plated at this time. On both sides it carried the name *Diamond* – as seen here – while on the bar side (largely devoid of windows) it was also named *Daffodil Bar* in 5¾in letters in a panel on the upper body side. It finally returned to the Southern Region in 1961 and was withdrawn in September 1963 – having probably seen little use as looks apparent from the picture. However, it was reinstated at the end of the following November and used by the London Midland Region as one of their Nightcap Bars on overnight services between Euston and Glasgow until late 1965. No renaming took place – just addition of 'The Nightcap Bar' roof boards. It was last seen in store at York in March 1966 and was broken up by Kings of Wymondham soon after. *R C Riley, courtesy Rodney Lissenden*

Utility Vans and Other Non-Passenger Coaching Stock

4

We now come to non-passenger coaching stock, ie vehicles built to run in passenger trains or at passenger train speeds but not actually carrying passengers. As far as the Southern Railway was concerned, this largely meant 'utility' vans. Van B stove No S398S is seen at Reading in October 1968, at the head of a van train hauled by a 'Crompton' diesel (later Class 33). This was built in September 1938, to SR Diagram 3093 and received its stove by at least 1944 – as indicated by the yellow eaves and guard's door panel on its otherwise rather dirty Southern Region green paint finish – pretty typical of the times. Nos 395-399 were the earliest recipients of stoves – although many more were so equipped later. Withdrawal date is March 1979, although some 30 continued to serve the South Eastern section until 1986 – the last being taken out of traffic in August/September of that year. A number entered departmental service and several still remain in such use. *M Rhodes*

The equivalent four-wheel guard's van was the Van C (coded BY after 1948). No 669 was completed in August 1938 and was photographed at Folkestone Harbour soon after, being shunted by ex-SER 'R1' tank No 1154. The van is to SR Diagram 3092 and is still in almost ex-works condition; the varnished teak droplight window frames contrasting with the Maunsell olive green finish and also with the travel-stained luggage van No 1152 (built in January 1937) coupled next to it. No 669 was one of a batch of 100 built between March and September 1938: Nos 651-750. However, they were not completed in numerical order as many of the underframes were built at Ashford and run to Eastleigh for bodywork assembly; this often resulted in a random order of construction. No 669 was actually built complete by Ashford Works and was one of the last to enter service. It ran until February 1972. Behind is one of the Southern Railway's own steamers with its characteristic yellowish-buff coloured funnel – this had a black top while the superstructure was white, with a black hull and red below the waterline. This livery was perpetuated by British Railways until replaced by rail blue era and later Sealink colours from 1965 onwards. *S Perrier*

Four – Utility Vans and Other Non-Passenger Coaching Stock

Just one 'BY' was rebuilt – No S938S – which was modified under order E5462 (dated 4 May 1965) and fitted with a lavatory in the former guard's compartment in June 1965 for GPO mail services between Waterloo and Portsmouth Harbour. Improved security requirements also dictated that the guard's door and the other droplights were planked in – notice how this has been done to blend in with the rest of the side planking. There is also a very small window high up to the left of the remaining double doors. Electric heating was added, probably in 1967. After modification both sides were identical and the van remained in use until December 1971. It was then retained pending further conversion to departmental use; this did not actually take place and the van was finally condemned in 1976, being broken up in the November of that year. It is seen in store at Micheldever in May 1976; despite appearances it is still in green livery. Built in January 1941, the original diagram number was 3092, amended to 3095 after rebuilding. Several of the unmodified vans have entered departmental service; at least eight became staff and tool brake vans numbered in the DB975XXX series in the early 1970s. These were repainted in the then current ED olive green livery. *P Fidczuk*

A small number of the standard luggage vans were also equipped with electric heating – for South Eastern and Central section passenger train workings. Nos 1537/58 were done in 1961 for the 'Golden Arrow' while Nos 1455/76/82/95/96/99, 1626/47 followed between 1964 and 1966. Freshly-repainted in rail blue, uneven-planked No S1476S is seen on a rush-hour Reading-Redhill train just after 5pm in the evening at Blackwater in the summer of 1967; the rest of the train is formed of a BR standard Mk 1 three-set in blue and grey livery. This van dates from May 1951 – one of a batch to SR Diagram 3103 built at the ex-LNWR shops at Wolverton – and was electrically wired in December 1966. The electrical connections may just be seen between the brake lever and the buffer. Note also the branding PMV (EW). Not long after it was air-braked and, along with the other nine vans, was transferred to the Western Region in 1973. It ran until 1976, finally becoming Eastern Region departmental van No DB975563 in September 1977. *M Rhodes*

Opposite top: Another exceptionally clean van from the same batch, No S1487 (now without 'S' suffix) at Ipswich on 5 June 1977. Not only are the ends painted rail blue but so are the headstocks, buffer shanks and solebars. This was also built at Wolverton, but in June 1951 and survived until April 1982, by which time withdrawals of these vans was occurring almost weekly; the last ones went just four years later. *P Fidczuk*

Opposite bottom: Breakdown packing van No ADS4 at Stewarts Lane in July 1985. A much older even-planked van, this was built in June 1935 as SR No 1189, but again to Diagram 3103. It was withdrawn in November 1953 after a relatively short traffic department life, becoming Signal & Telegraph van No DS4 at Hither Green. The addition of the end window dates from this conversion. It was later transferred to a breakdown van and repainted bright red – like the breakdown coach just seen behind and allocated to Stewarts Lane. The 'A' prefix indicates ownership by the CM&EE Department. Finally withdrawn in 1989, the vehicle put in far longer service as a departmental than as a passenger luggage van. *R C Riley, courtesy Rodney Lissenden*

Four – Utility Vans and Other Non-Passenger Coaching Stock

Similar Diagram 3103 luggage van No DS70021 in bright yellow at Hither Green on 25 September 1976. Another vehicle from the 1935/36 batch of 100 (actually 97 luggage vans and the three ferry vans), this was formerly No 1203, dating from May 1935, entering departmental stock slightly later in December 1958 – being renumbered in the BR DS70XXX series used from 1957 until 1971. As No DS70021 it was an Engineer's mess and tool van allocated to the Eastleigh district, moving to Hither Green later but seen all over the region with various track relaying machines – hence the yellow colour. It was condemned in February 1978 and broken up at New Cross Gate in the following October. *R C Riley, courtesy Rodney Lissenden*

Four – Utility Vans and Other Non-Passenger Coaching Stock

The true Covcar 'utility vans' with end doors (BR code CCT) were never as common as the luggage van equivalent (BR code PMV). This is No DS70202 awaiting delivery to the Bluebell Railway, which took place three days later, at Haywards Heath yard on 18 August 1974. To Diagram 3101, the van dates from May 1929 and was formerly SR No 2276. The livery may best be described as 'patchy' although during departmental service it was green with black ends. One of the vans fitted with removable fruit shelves when built, it may have been reserved for this traffic at various times of the summer – in particular from many country locations in Kent, Sussex, Hampshire, Dorset and Devon which specialised in soft fruit. Withdrawn in June 1963, the van entered departmental use as a stores van for the Mechanical Engineers, specifically for use between Eastleigh and Lancing Works, and was allocated departmental diagram No 1872. It was withdrawn from these duties in September 1973 and sold from Micheldever in August 1974. Currently it is being used by the Bluebell's signal & telegraph department, again as a stores van with only essential restoration being undertaken. *D Wigley*

An unidentified scenery van to SR Diagram 3182, at Reading on two different occasions during 1968. By this time theatrical scenery traffic had ceased and the vans were being used for ordinary parcels – so might turn up anywhere in the country. The number series ran from 4587-96, built in 1938, and 4597-4606, completed by BR in late 1949. Apart from No 4592, withdrawn in 1967, the rest ran until between 1976 and 1981. There was also an earlier batch, SR Nos 4577-86, built in 1928 on ex-LBSCR underframes and these differed slightly in detail so were allocated SR Diagram 3181. Their original LBSCR bogies were replaced by ones of LSWR pattern between 1932 and 1934, and these vans were withdrawn between 1959 and 1962. Some were used for Bertram Mills circus train and four (Nos 4584/89/98 and 4601) were equipped for carrying elephants. For this traffic they were provided with internal tethering rings, steel flooring and stronger springs – elephants are heavy! The left-hand picture shows the end doors and the high roof profile – useful for loading both theatrical props and elephants. *M Rhodes (both)*

Below: Former LMR Post Office van No S30276M at Dover in July 1971. One of four transferred to the Southern in that year, replacing some ex-GWR vehicles that had, in their turn, replaced pre-Grouping SECR vans on the service in 1960 (see page 28). This is a stowage van, unlike No S30291M illustrated in Plate 173 of *Southern Vans & Coaches in Colour*, which was a sorting van. They did not stay long on the Dover service as, by 1974, the six remaining Maunsell GPO vans had been released from the Waterloo-Dorchester/Weymouth run by the arrival of converted BR Mk 1 vehicles and these took over the Dover run until it ceased operating in late 1976. *M Rhodes*

Four – Utility Vans and Other Non-Passenger Coaching Stock

The Southern inherited just 96 special cattle vans from the pre-Grouping companies in 1923: 28 of LSWR origin (including one from the Somerset & Dorset Joint Line), 39 ex-SECR and 29 from the LBSCR. Of these, 35 were already some 30+ years old and in need of replacement. Their duties included conveyance of prize cattle to and from agricultural shows as well as circus animals and, of course, rather more mundane livestock duties as well. In 1929 a batch of 20 replacement vehicles was authorised; this was increased later to 50 vehicles and these were completed in the following year by Birmingham RCW. They were 26ft long and had a central compartment for the travelling groom, with stalls on either side for the animals. They were to SR Diagram 3141 and could easily be mistaken for a horsebox – and indeed they did carry horses on many occasions. To the Southern they were coded Catox – an abbreviation of the LBSCR term cattle box – but to BR they were SCV (special cattle vans). Numbers were 3679-3728 and they were lit by a single oil lamp in the roof, above the groom's compartment. Originally dual braked – to enable them to run anywhere in the country – the Westinghouse gear was removed from 1933 onwards. Ten more (Nos 3729-38) were completed by British Railways in 1952 to replace 10 pre-Grouping SR vans still in use at that time. These were identical save for the fact that they had electric lighting. The livery was originally SR olive green, changed to light grey during World War 2, although a few did receive malachite green from about 1939 onwards. After 1949 they received BR crimson lake – the livery still exhibited by No 3734 awaiting breaking up at Barry in September 1968, which indicates that it had not received a repaint for at least 12 years. This was one of the 1952 vans and was put into store in May 1966, being officially withdrawn in September 1967. This was quite typical for the times as many of the survivors hardly turned a wheel in revenue-earning service in the 1960s. Two were later rebuilt as train heating boiler vans and one of these appears on page 125. *M Rhodes*

BR-built van No S3736S actually on the move in a van train at Reading in 1967 – by then a rare sight. This has now received Southern Region green livery and dated from September 1952; it would have been outshopped originally in crimson lake and ran until October 1971 before being stored at Micheldever until condemned in August 1972. Quite a number of the 1930 vehicles were sent to Scotland in the late 1950s, presumably where some suitable traffic was still to be found and several of these were sold off from Inverurie Works in 1962/63, the bodies to be used as cattle sheds on Highland farms. All of the 1930 vans were officially withdrawn between 1961 and 1963 (most are recorded as December 1962), indicating they were already surplus to requirements by that time. The battery boxes for the electric lighting may be seen on the underframe; the dynamo was mounted on the other side. The four vertical shutters (two sets at each end) could be raised or lowered to control the amount of ventilation – here all four are in the open (lowered) position. *M Rhodes*

Four – Utility Vans and Other Non-Passenger Coaching Stock

Staying with the 'stored out of use' theme for a moment – here are three Diagram 3141 vans at Salisbury down yard in June 1968 where they sat for some time. All are from the 1952 batch and are likely to be Nos 3729/30/32 – withdrawn in 1970 and moved to Micheldever subsequently. Others were noted at Sturminster Newton and Blandford Forum, on the former Somerset & Dorset Joint line after its closure to passengers in 1966. The final van in BR stock was No 3733, withdrawn in August 1972 after at least a year of storage and this was sent to the former Pullman car workshop at Preston Park until 1978, when it was moved to York Museum for preservation. This proved a lengthy process but by 2004 the van was resplendent in Southern Region green livery and on display at Shildon. *M Rhodes*

5 Milk Tank Wagons

These were still non-passenger coaching stock but were a post-Grouping development. In 1923 milk was conveyed in churns in passenger-rated vans (a traffic still being handled by BR in the 1960s) but by 1930 increasing demand required the adoption of bulk transportation. The first milk tank wagons were short wheelbase four-wheelers but these were very soon found to be unsteady at the speeds needed for milk transportation so similar longer vehicles were introduced – the Southern completing nine of these in 1931. Success was still not achieved and six of the nine were reframed on six-wheel underframes in 1937/38 while all subsequent construction ran on six wheels. Opposite is a summary of the various types of SR milk tanks and trucks for carrying road tankers.

Above: No S4404 was one of the original six tankers, now to SR Diagram 3159 and was a 'milk tank type 1 converted'. Built originally for United Dairies' traffic as a Diagram 3152 four-wheeler in October 1931, it was reframed in November 1937, continuing in use until 1976. It is seen in store at Swindon after withdrawal, now showing ownership by Unigate Creameries. The former white livery still looks reasonably presentable. The tanks were always owned by the dairy and each had their own series of numbers; only the underframe was railway-owned. When built/rebuilt, the livery was silver, with vermilion red 'UniteD DairieS' lettering, together with the company initials 'SR' and generally the tanks were maintained in a clean external condition. Even by the 1950s this had given way to dirt – not necessarily guaranteed to inspire confidence in the internal cleaning standards. Most six-wheel tanks looked much the same – the exception being Diagram 3153 which had anchor-mounted tanks and no cross-beam at the vehicle ends. Dimensions were also fairly standard: all were 20ft 6in long over headstocks with a wheelbase of 6ft 6in + 6ft 6in. The four-wheelers were 21ft long with a 12ft wheelbase: standard RCH dimensions. *M Rhodes*

Five – Milk Tank Wagons

SR Classification	Diagram	Numbers	Vehicle type	Dairy	Remarks
Truck type 1	3151	4401-3	4w milk truck	CWS	Not replaced; withdrawn 12/38
Truck type 1 converted	3160	—	6w milk truck	CWS	CWS contract cancelled; (not built); Replacements built by GWR
Tank type 1	3152	4404-9	4w milk tank	UD	Reframed 1937/38; to D3159
Tank type 1 converted	3159	4404-9	6w milk tank	UD	Ex-D3152. Glass-lined tanks
Tank type 2	3153	4410-13	6w milk tank	EXD	Anchor mounted aluminium tanks
Truck type 2	3154	4414-18	6w milk truck	UD	For R A Dyson road trailers
		4425/26			Nos 4425/26 differ in detail
Tank type 3	3155	4419-24	6w milk tank	UDW	Glass-lined tanks
Tank type 4	3156	4427/28	6w milk tank	EXD	Stainless steel tanks
Tank type 5	3157	4429-32	6w milk tank	UDW	Glass-lined tanks
		4455-66		UD	Built at MWT request 1943/44
Tank type 6	3158	4433/34	6w milk tank	WP/EXD*	Glass-lined tanks
Tank type 7	3161	4435-42	6w milk tank	EXD	Stainless steel tanks
		4443-54		EXD	Built at MWT request 1943/44

*These two tanks ordered for West Park Dairy but taken over by Express Dairy before delivered.

Capacity of rail tanks 3,000 gallons, road trailers 2,000 gallons.

Milk tank type 3 No 4421 at Swindon Works around 1980. This was built at Lancing in October 1932 - part of a batch of six (Nos 4419-24) for United Dairies traffic between Wilts/Somerset and Vauxhall, to SR Diagram 3155. After a period of storage it was withdrawn in July 1981. Like all milk tank wagons still extant in January 1970, it was transferred from passenger to goods stock at that time; although just what this meant is unclear - possibly only a change in maintenance arrangements. *M Rhodes*

Tank No S4409 – another 'type 1 converted' but carrying a plate proclaiming Wilts United Dairies and, on the end, the tank number 606. It seems likely that SR/United Dairies tank numbers began at 601 and reached 628 by 1944, in the same order as their SR running numbers. This vehicle ran from November 1931 until either February 1937 or 1938 as a four-wheeler, then as a six-wheeler until December 1974, when it was purchased for preservation by the Great Western Society at Didcot – where it has since been restored to Express Dairy blue livery rather than white or silver UD livery as a result of sponsorship. The detail photographs below show close-ups of the centre axle box and very short brake lever – note the heavy spring dampers which were provided on all tanks from the early 1950s onwards – the tank mounting shackles with ladder and the cross beam/end stanchion supports. The raking support brace was a later addition. These detail views were all taken at Didcot in August 1978 before restoration commenced. *M Rhodes (all)*

Five – Milk Tank Wagons

At Bristol Temple Meads in the early 1970s is Diagram 3155 'type 3 tank' No S4424, looking smart in the livery of St Ivel, the only company that continued to take pride in the appearance of its tankers into the modern era. This illustrates another more recent development: the tilting of the tank to assist gravity, as opposed to pressure unloading (not that it improves the appearance). It also shows the alternative type of ladder/catwalk arrangement favoured by United Dairies on its later tanks. The running period spans October 1932 until March 1984, serving for the final few years as departmental water tank No DS4424. *M Rhodes*

Diagram 3157 'tank type 5' No S4431 at Swindon after withdrawal. This was built in September 1933 for United Dairies Wholesale division and carried silver livery with UDW lettering in green across the tank, eventually passing into Unigate ownership before withdrawal in July 1981. Most SR bulk milk traffic was concentrated on the West of England main line from Torrington, Lapford, Crediton, Seaton Junction, Chard Junction, Yeovil, Sherborne, Semley and Salisbury to bottling plants in south-west and south-east London but some came from Bason Bridge (Highbridge), Cole, Wincanton, Sturminster Newton and Bailey Gate via the S&DJR through Templecombe, the MSWJR from Cricklade at Andover Junction and also from Petersfield on the Portsmouth direct line, so it was quite a feat of organisation. Milk from locations nearer to London generally remained in churns until the traffic was lost to the roads. *M Rhodes*

Diagram 3158 'tank type 6' No 4434 is seen in Express Dairy ownership, possibly at Torrington *circa* 1968. This was ordered by West Park Dairy in September 1934 and would probably have carried its chocolate and cream colours had the company not merged with Express Dairy prior to delivery in April 1935, receiving instead the latter's standard blue livery with white lettering. This has the full height ladder and tank-top mounted catwalks favoured by Express. Note the initials 'SR' on the end beam with the tank number – 42 – in the centre. Express Dairy/SR tank numbers appear to be 9-12, 29, 30, 41, 42, 65-72 and 81-92 in the same order as their SR running numbers. This vehicle became departmental water tank No TDS4434 in July 1974. *E Hunt, courtesy P Fidczuk*

Five – Milk Tank Wagons

This is Express Dairy 'tank type 7' Diagram 3161 No S4440, possibly at St Erth in the early 1970s. One of 12 tanks built at the request of the Ministry of War Transport and Express in 1941 (the others were built by the GWR and LNER) to deal with increased wartime traffic, this ran from November 1942 until 1973. Just what livery it may have carried when new is not known – possibly the usual blue but maybe grey owing to wartime restrictions. Express Dairy did reinstate its colourful blue livery during the 1950s but by 1966 only a few tanks retained this livery. *M Rhodes*

During the latter part of World War 2 there was an even greater need for bulk transportation of milk – it was more efficient and utilised less labour than churns – so the Ministry of War Transport, in association with the Milk Marketing Board, ordered 24 more tanks with the Southern – and probably more elsewhere as well. These resulted in 12 extra type 7 tanks for Express Dairy (Nos 4443-54) and 12 extra type 5 for United Dairies (Nos 4455-66). These appeared in late 1943/early 1944 but were never actually taken into Southern Railway stock, being classed (and registered) as private owner wagons, with entries in the Southern Railway's private owner wagon register. They were eventually taken into BR stock on 11 January 1952. Type 5 tank No S4456 is seen in store at Swindon in the late 1970s, not long before being transferred to departmental use as water tank No DS4456 in January 1980. Something odd has happened to the tank number, visible on the end, as this should be 618 – it actually reads 861 so somebody has reversed the digits! Note that the wagon plate simply states the prefix 'S' rather than 'SR', reflecting the fact that these vehicles (or at least their underframes) were not owned by the railway until after Nationalisation. *M Rhodes*

Five – Milk Tank Wagons

Similar type 5 tank No S4464 at Newton Abbott in 1971 – plated for United Dairies Wholesale Ltd (as indeed was No S4456 in the previous photograph). Completed in 1944, No S4464 ran until September 1976. Tank number 626 is just visible on the end. Some sources state that towards the end some tanks were swapped about, but these pictures show no evidence of this. One type 5 tank has been preserved: 1933-vintage No 4430 based on the Bluebell Railway since 1981. *M Rhodes*

6 Pre-Grouping Wagons

We now return to the subject of the original book – wagons. At the Berry Wiggins plant on the Hundred of Hoo in 1964 we find another ex-LSWR Diagram 1310 round-ended open – very similar to SR No 4515 illustrated in *Southern Wagons in Colour* Plate 2. Photographer Mike Rhodes noted that there were about half-a-dozen of these on the site but only two could be readily identified. With the eye of faith the number is just discernible as SR 3209, ex-LSWR No 5595, built in 1908 and withdrawn on 22 June 1935. Clearly now in poor condition, it was a 10-ton, five-plank example of this most numerous diagram with Shepherd's patent axle boxes and Freighter brake gear. The last traces of Southern Railway brown livery remain, but all ironwork appears to have been blacked up; whether this was done by the Southern or after sale is not known. Note also the extreme overhang of the tar tank wagon to the right; this was probably an internal user around the plant, while to the left is a petrol tank wagon – probably from the Shell/BP fleet. *M Rhodes*

This LSWR Diagram 1541 goods brake van at Ryde St Johns on 14 August 1965 is one of the two 15-ton examples transferred to the Isle of Wight in May 1938. Formerly LSWR No 6532, built as a 10-tonner in 1904, it was renumbered as SR mainland No 54939 in February 1924. Upgraded to 15-tons and equipped with sanding gear (the sandpipes are just visible outside the wheels), probably at the same time, it was further renumbered to 56056 in February 1938, just prior to island transfer. Other modifications made then include insetting of the footboards – note the joggle of the supports just above the lower step – to clear the slightly restricted loading gauge of Isle of Wight lines. Livery is indeterminate; it may be SR brown with red ends under the grime. The van was withdrawn on 11 February 1967 along with all the other remaining ex-LSWR brake vans on the Island. *MBW collection*

Two of the 10-ton examples of Diagram 1541 at Newport on 4 October 1965, exhibiting rather different numbers. On the left is traffic department van 56055, illustrated and detailed previously in *Southern Wagons in Colour* Plate 98, while on the right is departmental No DS548 – actually branded S548. It may never have carried the correct DS number. This was formerly Island traffic van No 56054, transferred to departmental stock in June 1948, in theory to replace Isle of Wight Railway brake van No 472s on the weed killing train but, as this use was seasonal, the van could

often be seen being used as a normal traffic vehicle. Built in 1899 as LSWR No 5689, it was renumbered as SR mainland 54647 in January 1928, being further renumbered on transfer to the Isle of Wight in May 1932. Like all the other Island brake vans, withdrawal is recorded as 11 February 1967. Despite its slightly different status, the departmental livery was still light grey with black number patches – now somewhat degraded. Also see page 100. *M W F Gill*

Two views of Isle of Wight rebuilt Diagram 1541 brake van No S56047: on the left at Newport on 27 June 1960 and on the right awaiting breaking up in the former Freshwater yard at Newport on 14 June 1967. Maybe the van had not moved far in the intervening seven years? The light grey livery with black number patches shows up well on the earlier photograph while the later view shows the internal veranda end detail. Note also the Westinghouse through pipe, which was provided on all four rebuilds but not on any of the original vans. By the 1960s Nos S56047/49 were light grey, S56048 was in a washed out SR brown (see Plate 100 in *Southern Wagons in Colour*) while No S56044 had been withdrawn in May 1956 – believed still in SR brown but with black number patches. No new diagram number appears to have been allocated, but this is not the only instance where an island rebuild failed to be so recorded. It was probably immaterial as the vehicles would not be straying far. No S56047 dates from 1897 as LSWR No 11061; was renumbered as SR 54800 in December 1924 and again on transfer to the Isle of Wight in August 1928. Withdrawal was the usual February 1967. *D P Rowland/M Rhodes*

Six – Pre-Grouping Wagons

Opposite top: Another view of the 'one-ton van' on the Isle of Wight – at Ryde St Johns Road in the early 1960s. Previously illustrated in Plates 101 and 102 in *Southern Wagons in Colour*, this splendid-looking vehicle was much favoured for engineer's trains while on the island – as seen here. Just four of these were built in 1906, primarily for Nine Elms-Plymouth and Torrington goods services and the original general arrangement drawing shows a vehicle with six wheels. It is not believed they were built as such, but if so they did not run for long in that condition. Increased braking power was their *raison d'être* so perhaps the addition of a centre pair of wheels negated this by spreading the weight too much. Officially they were rated at 18 tons, but No S56058 was always marked 17-0 while on the Isle of Wight. It was renumbered from mainland No 54948 as early as October 1947, but was not actually transferred to the island until about May 1948 – being available a month or so previously to be included in the 'Ashford 1948' series of official photographs in which the red ends are very obvious. The van was later repainted in BR grey livery. Also visible behind are several ex-SECR 'Price & Reeves' dropside ballast wagons and, to the right, an LBSCR single bolster; both types were mainstays of the island departmental fleet. The bolster – No DS59045 (ex-LBSCR No 7317 of 1911 and later SR mainland No 58443) – is to SR Diagram 1616. This remained in BR stock until as recently as September 1994, although probably had not turned a wheel for years and is now preserved by the Isle of Wight Steam Railway. See pages 97-99 for more details of these bolster wagons. *T Cole collection*

Opposite bottom: An oblique view of a LSWR Diagram 1597 bogie bolster – No DS57872 at Guildford in May 1975 and loaded with substantial timber baulks; this was a very typical load for these wagons. This has lost its bolsters – in common with most of the survivors at that time – and was one of the final batch, being completed at Eastleigh in 1926 and entering departmental stock in March 1973. It was finally withdrawn in July 1978. The timbers are likely to be destined for a Civil Engineer's or a Permanent Way job. The livery appears to be light grey side rails but black otherwise. *M Rhodes*

Detail views of Diagram 1597 bolster 57872, taken on the same occasion. These show the Spencer's buffers, truss rod mounting, side roping rings and the LSWR 10in x 5in axle box. The diamond bogie wheelbase was 5ft 6in. Note also the last lifting date of 9/66 at station 4042 (New Cross Gate), rather indicating that the wagon was not repainted when transferred to departmental stock, while the next scheduled overhaul date is 6/77, which to judge from the withdrawal date, probably never took place. *M Rhodes (all)*

A 35-ton 'rectank', No 84019, seen at Longmoor on 1 May 1965. As the name suggests, these bogie vehicles were built towards the end of World War 1 for carrying tanks – most dating from 1918. At least 160 were completed by either private manufacturers or by various railway workshops for the War Department. Later the GWR, LMS and LNER inherited 40 each from some of their pre-Grouping constituents and most of these were subsequently equipped with two, three or four bolsters. Others, such as this one, remained with the Army while more were built as recently as the 1960s, but to almost the same design. This example was completed by the Lancashire & Yorkshire Railway in 1918 and was originally WD No 13101. It entered internal use at Longmoor Camp in June 1967. The steel framing under the buffers were for mounting jacks – used to steady the wagons as the tanks were rolled on and off. Left is a close-up of a diamond frame bogie from another rectank, seen on the same day. Although none were actually owned by the Southern, the proximity of the many Army bases meant that these wagons would be a regular sight on the SR. Longmoor, of course, had an extensive railway network served from both Liss, on the Portsmouth direct line and at Bordon, on the branch from Bentley. *M Rhodes (both)*

Diagram 1560 'dance hall' brake van No DS55491 in ED olive green livery at the most unlikely location of Barrow-in-Furness in 1985 – one of those wagons exiled from the Southern once it became a fully air braked region. Built in 1923 and allocated the SECR No 11935, this may never have been carried. It was transferred to departmental stock on 14 May 1960 and remained in service until 28 October 1987. TOPS code ZTO is carried, while the tare weight is recorded as 20.5t. Apart from a change of buffers and provision of instanter couplings, the van remains practically as built. *G Kent*

Similar Diagram 1560 brake No DS55497 at Watford Junction on 10 May 1980; this was one of those vans painted olive green that had weathered to an indeterminate purple brown colour. This still has the lettering in a box, but the TOPS code ZTO is clearly a later addition. It also retains the original tare weight of 25 tons. Handrails and lamp irons are picked out in white paint. Although the wagon plate is missing – probably now in the hands of a collector somewhere – the date of construction is correctly recorded on the solebar as 1927, making it one of the final batch of 20 built by the Southern Railway as order L110, dated May 1925 and completed at Lancing by the end of March 1927. The original self-contained buffers remain in place but instanter couplings are fitted; this was probably done after the van left the Southern Region. *P Fidczuk*

Ex-LBSCR 10-ton open No S27768 at Cowes on 21 August 1965. This was one of a batch of 75 transferred to the Isle of Wight in 1930. Built in 1926 as mainland No 19056, it was renumbered in May 1930 and never carried round ends, so was to SR Diagram 1364 from the start – although just as many were actually recorded as Diagram 1369, which strictly speaking was the round-ended equivalent. It was one of the last wagons to be completed at Lancing to an ex-LBSCR design. The livery may best be described as unpainted and whether it was still in use may be debated – the 10 tons load inscription has been painted out – but withdrawal is recorded as 15 October 1966. This high-level view shows the internal door detail. *M Rhodes*

Somewhat more colourful LBSCR open No S28299 is seen at Newport on 4 October 1965. This, at least, has some planks painted grey with black number patches, even if others have been replaced and remain unpainted. Clearly the door planks have suffered rather more from weathering, scuff marks and the like. Another 1926 Lancing build to Diagram 1364, mainland No 19042 (completed April 1926), this was a March 1929 transfer to the Island – from another batch of 75 sent over in that year. The instructions for these transfers includes 'round ends to be made square' so some older vehicles were sent as well as some of the most recent construction. Withdrawal is recorded as September 1959 but this must be wrong; perhaps it was then reinstated to survive until the end of steam operation. *M W F Gill*

Six – Pre-Grouping Wagons

This rather interesting picture was taken at Clapham Junction on Sunday 2 May 1965. The centrepiece is Waterloo & City line motor car No S57 en route to or from Stewarts Lane where bogie replacements were being made. Each car was taken from the line singly via the hoist alongside Waterloo station, out to Clapham Junction West London line platforms and then back to Stewarts Lane – this move generally taking place either on a Saturday afternoon or a Sunday – so this may be the return trip and the new bogies are in place. Certainly the shoe beams look to be new. This second generation of Waterloo & City Line stock dates from 1940; the cars being 47ft long, 8ft 7¾in wide and 9ft 7in high – they look pretty diminutive when seen out on the main line! SR Diagram 842 was allocated to the motor cars (Nos 51-62) while Diagram 846 applied to the trailers (Nos 71-86). Seating was for 40 third class (plus 60 standees) and 52 third class (plus 80 standees) respectively but doubtless any regular commuter on the line would tell you that the standing capacity could easily be exceeded. Their original livery was malachite and aluminium, later changed to rail blue and aluminium, then finally Network South East 'toothpaste stripe' from 1986. Bogie problems soon started but were dealt with by piecemeal repairs and partial replacements from 1947 until the 1960s. A complete programme of renewal began in March 1965, continuing until the following December. Car No 57 was delivered on 17 May 1940, probably running trials on the main line until commencing work underground at the end of October 1940. It was equipped with fluorescent lighting and a PA system in October 1986 – the only car done – and ran until 1993. It was brought to the surface for the final time on 29 May 1993, then being taken to MC Metals in Glasgow for breaking up, which took place a month later. Similar car No 61 is now preserved at York Museum.

The two match wagons fore and aft are ex-LBSCR five-plank opens – probably departmental Nos DS1596 and 1598 as both are listed as match trucks for the Waterloo & City line. They were converted in January 1941, then numbered 1596s and 1598s, ex-Diagram 1369 opens Nos 27516 (built in 1924) and 25787 (built in 1907 as LBSCR No 10720) respectively. For this purpose both had their drawgear and buffers at one end replaced by low-level underground-type couplings, to enable them to top and tail the tube cars on their journeys to and from works. Both had their round ends removed and were reclassified to Diagram 1364 in May 1942. Withdrawal is recorded as January 1966 – just after the completion of the bogie replacement programme. Both carry black livery with pale yellow lettering. The BR 20-ton goods brake at the right is No B955106, to BR Diagram 1/507 and built in 1961 while the SR 25-tonner on the left is an uneven-planked example of Diagram 1579 – No 56437 – dating from 1943 and withdrawn in July 1967. Motive power is provided by a BR Class 3 2-6-2T; possibly No 82018. *M W F Gill*

A rare survivor: an ex-LBSCR cattle truck seen at Newport in 1964. Built in 1922 as LBSCR No 7116 it was a 10-ton goods-rated cattle wagon and one of 420 owned by the LBSCR at Grouping. Allocated SR mainland number 53291 and Diagram 1528, it was transferred to the Isle of Wight in August 1927; Westinghouse fitted and then receiving the number 53374. It was one of six LBSCR cattle trucks sent over to cope with the anticipated level of cattle traffic on the Island. However, the traffic volume soon fell away and in August 1935 the vehicle was rebuilt into a covered goods wagon to SR Diagram 1457 for passenger's luggage in advance (PLA) traffic, and renumbered 46924. This number may just be seen roughly painted on the van at the far end. In March 1948 it was transferred to departmental stock as No 1066s, allocated to Newport as a Signal & Telegraph department stores van, which is where it spent most of the rest of its 'working' life, gradually losing all forms of identification – and its SR brown paint finish! Withdrawn in 1967, it was saved for the National collection and returned to the mainland and storage, firstly at Fratton and later Preston Park sheds. In 1977 it was returned to the Island, on long-term loan to the Isle of Wight Steam Railway and restored to its former PLA van condition. In June 2015 it was formally transferred to IWSR ownership and may be seen in their 'Train Story' exhibition at Haven Street, magnificently restored to SR brown with white lettering. Behind may be seen IWCR crane No 429s (seen in *Southern Wagons in Colour* Plate 155 on the same occasion) and ex-LSWR match truck No 429sm – both also now in the custody of the Isle of Wight Steam Railway at Haven Street. *M Rhodes*

Six – Pre-Grouping Wagons

An Isle of Wight Engineer's train approaches Smallbrook Junction behind 'O2' No 22 *Brading* on 6 August 1966. The train is topped and tailed by ex-LSWR brake vans – the leading vehicle being one-ton Diagram 1542 van No 56058 seen on page 90, now with its lookout glass covered by a piece of plywood, while at the rear are two Diagram 1541 vehicles; that in front still quite obviously exhibiting its SR red ends. Between are 12 ex-LBSCR single bolster wagons to Diagrams 1616/17 or 1619/20, carrying a mixture of SR and BR departmental red oxide or black liveries. Identification of these wagons is complicated as SR mainland and more recent island records fail to agree over which vehicles are to which type. Diagram 1616 was the shorter 12ft type, originally with a capacity of six tons, while the uprated eight- or 10-ton vehicles were to Diagram 1619. Diagram 1617 was the slightly larger 13ft six-ton version, while those uprated to 10 tons became Diagram 1620. Officially, island Nos 59033-36/46 were to Diagram 1617 while Nos 59037-45/47-52 were to Diagram 1616. SR Nos 59033-41 were originally ED allocated so received red oxide livery whilst Nos 59042-52 were traffic wagons and were painted brown. *R Hobbs*

Ex-LBSCR single bolster wagon No DS59041 at Newport on 2 April 1965, showing evidence of both BR black and SR red oxide liveries. This was built in 1909 as LBSCR No 7258 and was then of six tons capacity. It was renumbered as SR 58416 at Lancing in February 1927, to Diagram 1616. Renumbering to 59041 and uprating to 10 tons followed on 19 May 1928, with transfer to the Isle of Wight taking place a few weeks later. No change of diagram number appears to have been recorded to reflect the uprating. This was the last of the batch of nine originally destined for the Engineer's fleet, although once in BR numbering they were not necessarily prefixed DS and it appears that this was not always reinstated until they were returned exclusively to the Engineer's use on 23 July 1960. Final withdrawal took place on 1 April 1967 – probably after a busy final few months assisting with electrification works and the extensive repair of Ryde Pier. To the right is similar wagon DS59047, ex-LBSCR No 7203 of 1910, renumbered as SR mainland No 58382 in February 1926 and to the Isle of Wight in June 1928. This was a traffic department allocated wagon and shows no hint of red oxide livery. Its subsequent history mirrors No DS59041. Overhaul dates visible are from 1957, giving some idea of how long wagons might last between repaints. The Isle of Wight Steam railway now owns five of these wagons – Nos 59038/43/45/49/50 – three of which have been restored to Southern Railway colours. However, on arrival at Haven Street, Nos 59043/45 carried the numbers 59034 and 59046 underneath layers of paint, casting some doubt on the renumbering records. *M Rhodes*

Opposite top: A view of bolster wagons Nos DS59041/47, seen from above and taken on the same day. This shows details of the bolsters, chains and shackles as well as the mounting rings that allowed the bolsters to swivel on the truck – essential when traversing curves loaded with long timbers or rails. *M Rhodes*

Opposite bottom: Also part of the Isle of Wight departmental fleet in the 1960s were nine Diagram 1661 ex-LBSCR machinery trucks – although to the Southern Railway they were more accurately classified as road vehicle trucks. No DS60580 is also seen at Newport on 2 April 1965 in a livery that has a little of everything: faded SR brown side rails, black solebars and black departmental number/inscription patches. Built as LBSCR No 7149 in 1923 and one of 15 completed just after the Grouping, it never carried its allocated SR mainland number of 60538, going instead straight to Isle of Wight number on transfer there in July 1929. On the Isle of Wight their main use was conveyance of Chaplin's and Pickford's containers until this traffic was transferred to road haulage in 1936, after which half of the stock of road van trucks on the island were broken up. The rest found some use by the Engineer's until permanently transferred to them in October 1960. Withdrawal is recorded as May 1969. Sister-vehicle No 60579 is preserved at Haven Street. *M Rhodes*

Six – Pre-Grouping Wagons

Part of the Isle of Wight's weed-killing train at Newport on 12 February 1966. Water tanks Nos 443s and 428s are visible – neither of which ever carried their BR 'DS' prefixes. No 443s on the left began life as a 2,020-gallon tar tank for the Isle of Wight Central Railway and was one of two purchased for the sum of £100 from the Bute Works Supply Co of Cardiff in April 1898; this one being allocated the IWCR No 140. By 1923 both vehicles were in use between Newport and Medina Wharf, supplying water to the steam cranes employed there. At first allocated SR traffic department number 61383, in June 1928 it was transferred to departmental stock as No 443s, but continued to be used serving Medina Wharf. Following rebuilding of the wharf in 1930/31 it was fitted up as a weed-killing tank in February 1932. This must have proved a little unsatisfactory since just four months later the tank, with dimensions recorded as 13ft 7in long, 6ft 4in wide by 5ft 6in high (ie a slightly flattened cylinder) was remounted on the underframe of Isle of Wight Railway tar tank No 61381, which in turn received a second-hand ex-LSWR 18ft van underframe. In June 1949 this LSWR underframe was used to remount the tank from No 443s, bringing the vehicle to the condition seen in the photograph. The vehicle seen on the right, No 428s, was the other 1898 tank purchased from Bute Works Supply Co, IWCR No 141. This had a flat-topped 2,300-gallon tar tank, with dimensions of approximately 12ft long, 6ft 4in wide by 5ft 9in high. By 1923 this was already a water tank but was never allocated a Southern Railway traffic number, going instead straight to departmental No 428s. This joined No 443s in the weed-killing train in February 1932 but was similarly reframed four months later using the other IWR tar tank frame (from vehicle No 61382 which in its turn received another ex-LSWR van underframe), while in December 1950 this LSWR frame caught up with the tank of No 428s, giving some form of standardisation to the two vehicles. Both received red oxide livery in 1932, later black, but by 1966 the former colour was again showing through. Both vehicles were withdrawn in 1967 and broken up in the following year. Since 1948 they were supposed to run with Diagram 1541 brake 548s (page 89) but in practice any handy brake van was used for the weed-killing train. Note one small detail regarding the couplings: three-link at each outer end, screw couplings between the two tanks. The flat wagon on the left is the match truck for crane No 429s – No 429sm – also seen on page 96. *M Rhodes*

Taken from the down platform at Ryde St Johns Road on 31 July 1960, this shows a portion of Ryde Works, from where the entire Isle of Wight fleet was maintained since the early 1930s. In the centre is Isle of Wight Railway two-ton hand crane No 425s, an ancient specimen built by Kirkstall Forge Co of Leeds as long ago as 1865, making it one of the oldest items of rolling stock ever owned by the Southern Railway. Despite this, it put in a century of service and was finally retired in 1966, being rescued by its makers a year later and since preserved by them. Note the enormous octagonal-shaped jib. Behind this, under the sheer legs, is boiler trolley No DS439. Formerly Isle of Wight Railway carriage truck No 76; this was built (or possibly rebuilt) at Ryde in 1920, becoming SR No 4380 in the van list after the Grouping. It

Six – Pre-Grouping Wagons

was 22ft long and 7ft 6in wide with a capacity of 10 tons, but it is not believed a Southern diagram was ever issued for it. Converted into a boiler trolley in June 1930, then numbered 439s, its main duty was to carry boilers between the works and St Helens Quay for onward transportation to/from the mainland. Despite being a departmental vehicle, it was available to carry other loads on the island if necessary. It was classed as an internal user within Ryde Works after November 1952, although no new number in the 08xxxx series was allocated. The wagon was withdrawn and broken up in October 1966. Two ex-LBSCR Diagram 1364 opens at left and right, various wheelsets and other equipment complete the scene. *R Denison*

Two former Isle of Wight Railway van bodies long after being retired from railway traffic. The upper picture shows a van grounded on the trackside at Ryde St Johns, in use as a store and seen in 1964; that in the lower picture has been sold off and is seen on the waterfront between St Helens and Bembridge in 1967 – hence the lifebuoy. Neither may be positively identified and both were withdrawn prior to the Grouping – being about 18ft long or slightly shorter. Their 'new' replacements were built at Ryde Works between 1906 and 1920 – these being almost identical but about 2ft longer. This was a very common method of renewal at Ryde; existing ironwork being incorporated into new vehicles that were, essentially, larger copies of what they replaced. The Southern was clearly unimpressed with these vans since all 12 IWR covered goods vehicles were withdrawn in March 1927 – soon to be replaced by ex-LBSCR imports from the mainland. Surprisingly, a number of the earlier van bodies lasted for many years and it is believed at least two (maybe these two) have now been acquired by the Isle of Wight Steam Railway for eventual restoration. *M Rhodes (both)*

Also grounded on The Duver at St Helens around 1926 was this former goods brake van. Clearly of LBSCR Stroudley origin, it was one of four sold to the Isle of Wight Central Railway in either 1902 (its Nos 1-3) or 1907 (No 4). Numbers 1-3 are recorded in Brighton registers as being ex-LBSCR Nos 136/38/39 – all built in 1877 and sold in July 1902 – but the former identity of the fourth vehicle is unclear; it might be ex-LBSCR No 124, 141 or 165. In 1913 the uneasy working relationship between the Isle of Wight Central and the tiny Freshwater, Yarmouth & Newport Railway came to a head and the latter then decided to work its own railway with stock hurriedly procured thereafter. Amongst the stock purchased was one goods brake, which must have been IWCR No 1 or No 4, which became No 13 in the FYNR fleet (FYNR Nos 1-12 were coaching stock). It was vacuum-piped for use in the line's mixed trains. The FYNR directors clearly remained in a belligerent mood as this was the only one of the pre-1923 Southern companies to dispute the terms of the Grouping Act, resulting in the company not being absorbed into the Southern proper until August 1923. The brake van then became SR No 56038 but, like ex-LBSCR brake vans of similar vintage on the mainland, the vehicle was not destined to survive for very long; it was withdrawn on 20 March 1926 and it may never have carried its allotted Southern number. It was soon sold off and grounded, where it almost certainly remains to this day, albeit not now looking so presentable. The picture was taken in 1967. *M Rhodes*

Post-Grouping Wagons

7

The Southern's most numerous wagon – the eight-plank open goods – of which there were 11,650 of various types, representing almost one third of the wagon fleet. This may sound like a lot of wagons but compared to the LMS and the LNER it was a pretty small total. Even the most numerous pre-Grouping wagon design (the ex-Midland Railway Diagram 299 five-plank) numbered over 63,000 examples so, while the Southern scored on passenger traffic densities, it was a long way behind in terms of goods traffic. Open No S26726 is seen at Kings Lynn in 1985; this was a very early example of a 10ft wheelbase 'rebuild type 4' to SR Diagram 1400 and dates from August 1936. It would have been built with second-hand ex-SECR wheelsets, giving it a capacity of 10 tons and was unfitted. At some point subsequent to construction new (or at least newer open-spoke) wheels were provided, allowing uprating to 12 and later, in World War 2, to 13 tons. Once in BR ownership, vacuum brakes in conjunction with Morton brake gear and new buffers were eventually provided, as well as replacement axle guards and channel steelwork to replace the two lower end planks. This last was to prevent loads from bursting out through the ends and was a very common BR modification on all open wagons irrespective of origin. The wagon entered departmental use as long ago as December 1965, which may be when the inscription 'Not to be used for PW ballast or other Engineer's materials' was applied. It was easy to overload these wagons with such materials and the cupboard doors were then liable to burst open under load – hence the instruction. Some wagons were cut down to five or even four planks high to overcome the problem. The livery is fitted wagon bauxite, while the last overhaul date of '1-10-63' is visible on the solebar. By the time the picture was taken the vehicle was condemned, having been used as a barrier wagon around Kings Lynn docks for some years. *G Kent*

A smart-looking Bulleid five-plank open to Diagram 1389; however, this would have been 1375 when the wagon was built in 1943 with the change resulting from the provision of vacuum brakes in the 1950s. This was one of the wagons originally planked up using 1½in thick hardwood – typical of many built between 1943 and 1948. Photographed at Guildford in September 1972, No DS5845 now has more modern buffers and axle boxes and carries Engineer's olive green livery. It entered departmental use in August 1964 and was condemned in March 1982. For much of that time it was allocated to the Signal & Telegraph department at Guildford. *M Rhodes*

Another Diagram 1389 open from the same batch – No ADS5820M – shows a curious form of prefix and suffix lettering normally only confined to carriage stock. In contrast to the last picture, this wagon looks extremely run-down with many replacement unpainted planks, patch paint and evidence of repairs. Note also the part white-painted diagonal strap – normally the indicator of an end-door wagon! However, despite vacuum-fitting and the provision of BR axle guards the rest of the underframe remains substantially in original condition, including the axle boxes, while the original buffers have been extended. The vehicle dates from 1943 and entered departmental stock in November 1984 – not long before being photographed at Warrington. Final withdrawal date is not known. *G Kent*

A traffic department Bulleid five-plank in bauxite, No S13053 at Eastleigh in September 1966, labelled 'Loco5X' indicating use for loco coal, maybe for five trips only, probably for Eastleigh shed. This dates from March 1948 – another Diagram 1375 wagon with 1½in hardwood planks, but in this case the middle three were not originally bolted in place; an economy that proved rather short-lived. Vacuum-fitted by BR and rediagrammed to 1389, it now has modern Oleo buffers, Morton brake gear, fabricated axle boxes and Instanter couplings. Withdrawal came not long after – in May 1967 – probably after completing its five scheduled trips with loco coal. *M Rhodes*

Another Bulleid Diagram 1389 open – No S13957 – this time at Reading in August 1968. Bauxite livery with lettering in panels and evidence of one patch repair with a metal plate. Built in September 1948 and then one of the last true Bulleid Diagram 1375 wagons, this had softwood planking with just the top and bottom plank of the drop door in hardwood. Although now vacuum-fitted and with different axle boxes, this wagon retains its original buffers, with shanks having been extended by collars welded on to them, to suit the screw couplings. Withdrawal came in May 1981 – the wagon remaining a traffic department vehicle throughout. *M Rhodes*

A pair of early British Railways 13-ton shock-absorbing wagons – a development of the final Southern design to Diagram 1392 – seen at Grimsby in 1985. The Dock Office clock tower may just be seen in the background. Numbers are KDB720788/721167; these were part of a batch of 800 built at Ashford in 1950, to BR Diagram 1/035. Prefix K denotes vehicles allocated to the Signal & Telegraph Department. No 720788 was originally unfitted, No 721167 was vacuum-braked from new. Both differ in details such as buffers and in livery, while the far wagon has been partially resheeted using planks from a former unfitted wagon. Only a few planks still exhibit the three white vertical stripes to denote a shock-absorbing wagon. *G Kent*

Seven – Post-Grouping Wagons

One of Bulleid's infamous five-plank dropside wagons to BR Diagram 1/033, No B483723, seen at Surbiton in October 1970. One of 100 completed at Ashford Works in late 1949, they were rejected by the traffic department on account of the difficulty in raising the heavy dropside door back into place, so were passed to the Civil Engineer instead – the thinking being that there would always be sufficient manpower on hand to raise the doors. However, this example only just carries the 'On loan to CCE' branding (to the right of the white box) and is loaded with scrap metal, so perhaps is now in traffic use. Two sets of lettering may just be seen on its rather washed-out black or creosote livery – the original on the bottom plank, the later in the panels. Although it now has Instanter couplings, it remains unfitted and was probably withdrawn soon after being photographed. *M Rhodes*

Some vehicles in the Southern Region internal user series were drawn from the other companies, former private-owners or from BR stock. Internal user No 081581 has an interesting pedigree – and also an incorrect number! Seven thousand of these slightly odd-looking mineral wagons were built in 1944 to a Metro-Cammell design for use in France following D-Day; however, by 1950 maybe SNCF found them less-than-ideal and was keen to return them. British Railways was then desperately short of modern wagons so was equally happy to oblige. Towards the end of 1950 the wagons began to reappear on British soil, to be reconditioned and enter service for BR. A total of 6,982 were put back into traffic (presumably the other 18 were either lost or declared unserviceable), for which BR Diagram 1/112 was allocated. Here they received BR number plates but showing a build date four years prior to the existence of British Railways! They proved less than perfect here as well for, like the SR eight-plank opens with cupboard doors, these also had a nasty habit of bursting open when loaded, so the vehicles were eventually restricted in their use. Many were later sold to industry or the National Coal Board, while others became departmental stock. According to the records, No 081581 was an ex-LNER wooden-bodied mineral wagon allocated to Southampton Docks, whilst No 081531 was an ex-SNCF mineral allocated to Littlehampton (ex-BR No B195795 in June 1967 and withdrawn in June 1973). As the picture was taken at Littlehampton in 1970, it is suggested that this is the wagon in question but exhibiting an incorrect number. *M Rhodes*

Opposite top: Staying with the theme of different origins for a moment, this is an RCH 12-, later 13-ton, eight-plank mineral wagon, seen at Guildford in January 1967, labelled 'Loco5X' in the same manner as the Bulleid open seen previously on page 105. Under the dirt it is also marked 'Cond' with a date of '20-6-63' so its fate is already sealed. This was one of a batch of 100 wagons built by Derbyshire Carriage & Wagon Co for the Great Grimsby Coal, Salt & Tanning Co in 1936, its Nos 1086-1185. This was formerly No 1105, registered by the LNER as its PO wagon entry No 9813 and, like almost all mineral wagons, was pooled from 1 September 1939, allowing it to be used by any trader. Taken into British Railways stock after 1948, it received the number P266791. The original livery was black, with white lettering – the large words 'Coal' and 'Salt' being shaded red. Traces of this are still visible nearly 30 years after its owners lost possession. The red planks at the lower left are a more recent repair with second-hand timbers taken from another wagon. The Great Grimsby Coal, Salt & Tanning Co had diverse interests, including rope and twine manufacture, engineering, tanning and coal merchants. It had depots along much of the East Coast but also had an office at Poole and another at Padstow from which it supplied many trawler fleets, so its wagons may have been seen on the Southern Railway. The author is grateful to David Larkin and John Arkell for information on this company. *M Rhodes*

Seven – Post-Grouping Wagons

Below: At Surbiton in October 1968, two years earlier than B483723 on page 107, is Diagram 1383 Conflat D No S39553, in bauxite livery. This dates from late 1932 and was vacuum-fitted from new. Half of the class of 150 were originally unfitted and these were originally coded Conflat C, but it was soon found advantageous to equip all SR container trucks with vacuum brakes. The Conflat Ds could carry two containers back-to-back but, by the 1960s, were more often used to load cars – especially the (then described) invalid carriages built by AC Cars of Thames Ditton which probably explains its presence at Surbiton, especially as wheel chocks may be seen on the wagon. Withdrawal is recorded as 20 February 1971. Note how busy Surbiton yard then was – but not for very much longer. Inevitably it is now the station car park. In the background is a Southern Covcar (CCT); this was one of a pair used there by the Commercial Department as stores vans from April 1967. They were internal user Nos 082788/90, formerly utility vans Nos 2399 and 2457. *M Rhodes*

Tank wagons were the largest class of wagon to be excluded from the Government pooling scheme of September 1939 – they were rather too specialised to be released for general use – so they continued to run and display individual liveries right through to the modern era. Shell/BP 10-ton tank No 75 is an elderly example on a timber underframe, seen at Guildford in 1964. This was built by the Midland Railway Carriage & Wagon Co as long ago as 1898, to one of its standard designs at 18ft in length. Similar examples were built for a number of other operators. It was registered by the LNWR – its registration No 22081 – although the original owner is not known. Identical tank No 74 was built at the same time. By World War 1 it was part of the BP fleet and this merged with Shell Mex in 1932 – the original BP wagons retaining their old numbers. It was withdrawn in 1966. The author wishes to thank Peter Fidczuk for this information. *M Rhodes*

Opposite top: Not exactly Southern wagons either – but very much a part of the North Kent railway scene. Two Blue Circle cement vans are seen at Swanscombe cement works in 1963. This was served off the down side of the line between Greenhithe and Northfleet and was originally provided for the Associated Portland Cement Manufacturers (APCM), later part of British Portland Cement Manufacturers (BPCM), later still owners of the Blue Circle emblem, which had its own fleet of locomotives for shunting within the complex which extended for some distance on either side of the railway. Private-owner vans were always a rare breed and were mostly confined to breweries, lime, salt and cement companies. Van No 133 carries the Blue Circle Portland Cement logo and a liberal coating of cement dust (as did most of the surrounding area!) but is clearly now out of service as it no longer has any doors. Van No 132 on the right carries the brand name 'Ferrocrete' but both carry 'Non-Pool' inscriptions to indicate that vans were never part of the post-September 1939 pooling arrangements that otherwise applied to ordinary privately-owned mineral wagons. They are likely to be 16ft long over headstocks and 7ft 6in wide, with a wheelbase of 9ft. The attractive pale yellow and blue livery dates from 1948 – prior to then cement vans were usually either grey or a light red-brown colour. Above and behind an aerial ropeway conveying skips crosses the site. Thanks are again due to David Larkin and John Arkell for information. *M Rhodes*

Seven – Post-Grouping Wagons

Right: A Maunsell/Lynes covered goods wagon – with the characteristic semi-elliptical roof profile that identifies any Southern van from those of the other companies. This is one of the 9ft wheelbase, 10-ton examples to Diagram 1429 with second-hand LSWR wheelsets and axle boxes. Engineer's van No DS44637 was photographed at Ashford Works in October 1968. Built in late 1931, this was one of 450 that were originally unfitted and had 'Freighter' brake gear. A further 150 were built with vacuum brakes, and a few of the unfitted wagons were so equipped during BR days. Despite still being without vacuum brakes, this van is painted bauxite and entered departmental stock on 12 May 1962, being withdrawn in August 1971. The left-hand axle box cover is a William Panter standard; that on the right to Shepherd's patent. Even after nearly 40 years, the van remains almost as built. *M Rhodes*

111

A long-term departmental van to Diagram 1458, painted very faded olive green – indeed it could almost be unpainted timber – seen at Eastleigh Works on 20 April 1975. This was built as SR No 49032 in late 1937 and was a 10ft wheelbase 12-ton example with two 15in vacuum cylinders and Morton brake gear – the clutch mechanism of which is clearly visible. It entered departmental service as soon as September 1947, renumbered as 541s, to work between Eastleigh and Ashford Works, carrying stores items for the Chief Mechanical Engineer's department. Later becoming No DS541, then No CDS541, its duties subsequently took it to and from York for British Rail Engineering Ltd instead of Ashford. It became internal user No 083505 at Eastleigh in May 1985 and was finally withdrawn in December 1989. When photographed it had received more modern axle boxes but was otherwise as built. *M Rhodes*

A wagon from the same batch as No CDS541 but still in ordinary traffic: No S49196 is seen at Guildford around 1967. Built in December 1937 to Diagram 1458, this wagon now has lettering in panels on its bauxite finish. Here we see the opposite side with the direct-acting brake lever. Withdrawal is recorded as March 1970. *M Rhodes*

Another Diagram 1458 van, but from the next batch built between November 1938 and October 1939. These were not completed in strict numerical order but the change to uneven (2+2) planking occurred during this period. No DS49345 was one of the final even-planked examples, seen at Guildford in May 1970 coupled to ballast cleaner No 7 (the yellow-painted vehicle on the right). The van has only been patch-repainted on transfer to departmental stock – with olive green panels to cover the previous traffic department lettering, leaving the faded bauxite finish elsewhere. The van retains its vacuum brakes (denoted by the red-painted pipe on the end) and is another Morton-braked example with two 15in vacuum cylinders. Withdrawal date is not known. *M Rhodes*

Uneven-planked Diagram 1455 van No CDS65791 at Eastleigh in company with No CDS541 (see page 112) on 20 April 1975. The prefix 'C' has clearly been added outside the panel and denotes ownership by British Rail Engineering Ltd. The livery is very faded bauxite, with the instruction 'To work between Eastleigh Works and Ashford Works' added on the side. Diagram 1455 was the wartime 'austerity' version of Diagram 1458 and these were unfitted when built. Vacuum brakes were added by BR from the 1950s, when the existing buffers were extended with collars welded to the shanks. Replacement axle boxes have also been provided. Built in 1943, this van was withdrawn in April 1979. *M Rhodes*

Southern Rolling Stock in Colour

A Diagram 1455 van built at Ashford for the Great Western in 1942 (GWR Diagram V35) is seen at Reading about 1970. No W144525 bears an overhaul date of March 1966 but has recently been much replanked and patch-painted since then, as a lot of the original 2+2 timberwork has been replaced by even-planks. The lettering in panels is also more recently applied. More modern buffers and axle boxes have also been provided. Note the various destinations exhibited. These include Slough, Maidenhead (MHD), Wrexham, Stockport and Manchester. *M Rhodes*

Plywood sheeted van No S54431, again at Reading possibly on the same day as No W144525. The plywood vans were to SR Diagram 1452 and construction spanned the period from 1945 to 1950. This is an early example, running from 1945 until August 1971 and would have been unfitted when built. Freighter brake gear was usual on this diagram. The heavy self-contained buffers are BR replacements of the originals, while the right-hand axle box is of LNER pattern. Chalked destinations visible include Whitehaven and Worcester. *M Rhodes*

Seven – Post-Grouping Wagons

Extreme weathering is apparent on this BR-built van to Diagram 1452 – in fact BR Diagram 1/202 was allocated to these final vehicles. No B752912 was completed in late 1949 but had vacuum brakes from the start – many did not. One 18in vacuum cylinder was provided in conjunction with the SR 'Monarch' brakes and the off-set vee hanger. This still has its original axle boxes but has the 1947 axle guards – which may have provided when built. Long (1ft 8½in) buffers are evident to suit the screw couplings. An overhaul date of 11/69 is visible at top left and the vehicle was already withdrawn when photographed around 1972. *M Rhodes*

Banana traffic through Southampton Docks was always important but the Southern relied on its existing stock of ex-LSWR vehicles until 1933. In that year the traffic increased markedly so a number of vans were hired from the LNER and, two years later, 200 vans were built to this design. SR numbers were 50575-774, so this was the last of the batch – completed in December 1935. Diagram 1478 was allocated and they ran on a 10ft wheelbase underframe with 'power' brake gear; this had one centrally-mounted 18in vacuum cylinder and eight brake blocks. Before 1940/41 they carried stone buff livery with venetian red lettering but, during the war, some at least received red oxide with lemon yellow lettering. Banana traffic practically ceased for the duration and the vans were used for meat traffic instead. No doubt some lasted right through in very dirty buff livery. After 1948 they were repainted bauxite, while the yellow spot was added between 1961 and 1963 and indicated increased levels of insulation. The picture was taken at Southampton Docks on 22 April 1967 – just four months before withdrawal. *M Rhodes*

The final batch of banana vans were required in a hurry, as the LNER wanted its vans back from hire, so 125 ordinary covered goods wagons that would have otherwise been completed to Diagram 1458 were altered as additional banana vans – to Diagram 1479. These were Nos 50775-899 and appeared between April and July 1938. Unlike Diagram 1478, these resembled the ordinary vans with the semi-elliptical roof profile – they just had different doors, no end vents and greater levels of insulation, resulting in their tare weight being about two tons heavier. 'Power' brake gear was again provided. No S50879 was photographed at Southampton Docks, again on 22 April 1967, and lasted for just three months longer. The yellow spot marking was added between 1961 and 1963 when steam heating was discontinued in favour of greater levels of insulation. *M Rhodes*

A left-hand ducket 25-ton goods brake van, No DS55979 at Temple Mills yard (Leyton, East London). One of the earliest examples of SR 'pillbox' brake vans, this was built in 1928 on an underframe of SECR design also used under the 'dance hall' brakes (see page 93). It is typical of those built from April 1928 until week ending 2 October 1929. The tare weight of this example is now 20.0t and the TOPS code is ZTO – the same as the ex-SECR design vans. The sandboxes have been removed – a process that started not long after World War 2. It entered departmental use as long ago as April 1964 and would have been exiled from the Southern Region in 1978 as it was not air-braked or piped. The picture was taken on 14 October 1992 but the van still exhibits its last overhaul date of May 1977 and is one of the olive green repaints that has faded to brown livery. Final withdrawal is recorded as 20 March 1990 so whether it is still in use or awaiting disposal is not known; however, it is coupled to a 'Grampus' ballast wagon so may still be in service. *M W F Gill*

For comparison, here is a right-hand ducket van to Diagram 1579 – as built from week ending 9 October 1929 onwards. This also has the later style of rather lighter stepboard brackets. No DS56249 is seen at Plymouth in September 1975, still carrying its SR-applied unfitted grey livery. It is allocated to Westbury, for the use of the Western Region District Engineer, so may have been inherited from the Southern Region since the boundary changes of January 1963. This van was built in 1933 and lasted until November 1985. Note that it is still rated at in excess of 25-tons and the inner veranda end is painted very faded cream or stone colour. *M Rhodes*

Exceptionally smart Diagram 1582 25-ton brake van No S55659 is seen at Sidmouth on 24 July 1958, having just been repainted in fitted stock bauxite livery with the upper veranda end in cream. It is actually through-piped rather than vacuum fitted – the vacuum pipe to the guard's release valve being seen running vertically up the side of the van. Diagram 1582 vans, dating from December 1947 to November 1948, were uneven-planked and were without sandboxes from the start. They also had a modified form of brake gear designed to even up the pull on all eight brake blocks – a failure of the earlier designs. Note also that an additional end window has been provided, making these vans much lighter inside the guard's compartment. Many were actually one or two tons lighter in weight than the rated amount, but No S55659 tares just 1cwt below the 'correct' figure. This van was completed in mid-1948, running until December 1967. *R C Riley, courtesy Rodney Lissenden*

One of the 40 SR brake vans built for the War Department in 1941/42, is seen at Longmoor in June 1967, carrying Army drab (green) livery. No AD49022 was one of the original batch of 20 completed at Lancing in September 1941 and registered as a private owner wagon in the Southern's PO wagon register: entry No 1010. Originally numbered B2 by the Army (presumably in a separate number series just reserved for brake vans, although this is not confirmed, B1-B4 being the only numbers known), in March 1942 it received the number WD11003. By 1956 it was at Longmoor carrying the number 49022, where it remained until the line closed in 1969. Eventually purchased by the Kent & East Sussex Railway, it was restored in 1982 and given the pseudo SR number 56495 (No 56494 being the highest numbered SR Diagram 1579 vehicle). It was restored for a second time in 2006 and then numbered M360327 – the number taken by one of the two ex-Shropshire & Montgomeryshire vans inherited by BR in 1949 – but not this actual van. There are some detail differences compared with contemporary Diagram 1579 brakes but the most obvious are the two vacuum cylinders mounted on the end platform. A through Westinghouse pipe was also provided. This low-level view shows the plate-backed axle guards and brake rigging to advantage. *M Rhodes*

By the mid-1930s some of the pre-Grouping lighter brake vans (generally 10-tons or thereabouts) were beginning to show their age and so a batch of 50 15-ton versions of the standard 'pillbox' were produced; these were mounted on a 10in channel instead of the heavier 15in channel underframes used on the 25-ton vans. No S55679 is seen at Bournemouth East Goods on 28 June 1960, in unfitted grey livery with black number patches. The inner veranda end looks to be bauxite and cream, although officially the colours were purple brown and stone – separated by a 1½in black band. The latter is most definitely not present. Diagram 1581 was allocated and the running period spans August 1934 to September 1967. Note that this is another 15-ton van that has lost its sandboxes – most of the lighter vans retained them to the end. By the 1950s most vans were allocated to a specific duty or branch line – this one just states 'Not in Common Use'. *D P Rowland*

Seven – Post-Grouping Wagons

At the other end of the brake van spectrum we have 'Queen Mary' bogie van S56304 in the unlikely location of Romford coal yard on 3 March 1978. This is also marked up 'Not in Common Use' but is correctly painted bauxite with the lettering in panels. The yard at Romford was approached down a steep gradient from the main line (seen in the background) so this may be the reason for its use. This was to Diagram 1550 and dates from August 1936 – one of those with fully planked rather than steel-sheeted side panels. It appears to have been one of the earlier withdrawals – perhaps not so long after being photographed. *P Fidczuk*

Diagram 1550 van No S56289 in the up yard at Yeovil Junction on 27 February 1965. This has the two middle panels covered in steel sheet – as did at least 12 of the 25 examples of the class by this time. It is also lettered 'Not in Common Use' as were most of the vans during the 1960s and early 1970s. It was only later that they seem to have 'escaped' to other regions of British Railways. This example became DS56289 on 21 May 1977 and was withdrawn on 28 February 2002, subsequently being purchased by the Swanage Railway. It has been restored to BR bauxite livery and is currently operational. Items of note behind the van include a 25-ton 'pillbox' in light grey and what appears to be a former milk tank wagon in the service of a soil fertiliser company. Its red-painted road tanker may just be seen behind the 'Queen Mary' and the tank wagon is lettered '………Company' in the same red lettering. No further information about this wagon or the company has been found. The departmental coach to the left is of Great Western origin. *M W F Gill*

A more recent picture of a Diagram 1550 brake van: No ADS56299 is seen at Snowdown Colliery sidings in October 1989, carrying 'Dutch' grey and yellow livery and allocated to the Mechanical Engineer's. Snowdown Colliery closed in 1987 but the sidings were used for wagon storage during the construction of the Channel Tunnel, which is the reason for the vehicle's presence. The van has lost its sandboxes and is TOPS coded YTX. It has replacement buffers and was Westinghouse fitted as long ago as June 1961 but this has proved useful for its present-day role working with high-capacity modern wagons; one of which may just be seen. Transfer to departmental stock occurred in August 1978 and by 2000 the van was painted in very smart EWS red and yellow livery. It was finally sold for preservation to Peak Rail at Matlock, arriving there in 2011. *M W F Gill*

Clearly just ex-works, this is extremely smart and colourful van No ADS56303 at Dover on 3 May 1988 in Railfreight Construction Sector two-tone grey with logo, yellow ends and orange roof stripe. Nobody from the Southern Railway era would have predicted what a colourful future lay in store for some of these brake vans! Built in August 1936, it was another of the six Diagram 1550 vehicles equipped with Westinghouse brakes in 1961 for continental freight traffic to and from Hither Green yard. By the 1970s, it was in use for electrification works on the London Midland Region and received yellow and black chevron pattern ends. Finally withdrawn in August 2006, it is now owned by the Dean Forest Railway, arriving there with heavy self-contained oval-head buffers and not those seen in the picture. It has yet to be restored. *Rodney Lissenden*

Seven – Post-Grouping Wagons

In the rather bleak surroundings of Grangemouth Docks in 1984 is Diagram 1598 'Borail' No S57937, by then in internal use. This was built in October 1943 – the last vehicle on order A1282. This batch retained diamond frame bogies but had oval buffers – those built in 1936/37 had round buffers. The wagon has lost its bolster stanchions (they may be lying in the bed of the wagon) but retains traffic department grey livery and is still marked as 40 tons capacity. It was withdrawn from ordinary service in January 1973. How long it survived in internal use is not known. *G Kent*

Diagram 1681 machinery truck/lowmac No DS61098 is seen at Andover Junction on 10 September 1967 – standing partly inside the goods shed. This was an ex-SECR Lionel Lynes design that did not appear from Ashford Works until after the Grouping. However, this example was constructed at Eastleigh (as recorded on the wagon plate) in 1928 (order E109). It entered departmental use in July 1965 and was withdrawn in March 1996. It still carries unfitted stock grey livery with black number patches – the D of DS clearly being a later addition. It has several chocks and mounts on the wagon bed and also has timber upstands at each end; this was a feature of several of these wagons during their departmental service. Also of interest behind is the SR platform barrow. This is one of the older type with 10-spoke wheels; later ones featured disc wheels. *M Rhodes*

Two Diagram 1681 machinery trucks at Lowestoft in 1986. Nearest is No DS61160 while behind is No DS61154. Both date from June/July 1942 and were part of an order for 22 additional wagons completed at Ashford under order A1096. They are painted olive green, are TOPS coded ZXR and labelled 'Lowmac'. Built as 20-tonners, they were uprated to 21 tons almost as soon as they were completed. Both are now air-piped and are loaded with Civil Engineer's Donelli single line track relaying units – Nos 78414 and 78415. Both wagons entered departmental service on 28 April 1965 – then on the Southern Region but moved elsewhere in the 1970s. Withdrawal dates are March 2001 for No DS61160, May 2002 for No DS61154. *G Kent*

Track ballasting is in progress at Crowthorne in August 1966. Diagram 1772 40-ton hopper No DS62029 is in the centre of the view; this is one of the original SR lot ordered from Metropolitan Carriage, Wagon & Finance Co in 1928/29 with control wheels at one end only. From this viewpoint the central stiffening strut may just be seen. This was actually the last of the batch (numbers were 62005-29) and lasted until March 1975. Another identical hopper is seen behind and on both the operator is opening the control wheels to let the stone out through the bottom centre doors. This was a matter of fine judgement by both those on the wagons and the train crew; too little stone or too fast a pass and the run would have to be repeated, too much stone or too slow a speed and the material would pile up under the

wagon – at worst leading to a derailment. Not quite so difficult if done in daylight, but at night and in wet conditions… The far hopper is one of the 1947 batch (Nos 62055-74) on cast AAR bogies – note the different shape of the hopper end – and these had control wheels at both ends, operating the doors over one half of the wagon from each; allowing far greater control and precision in placing the stone. The wagon in the near foreground is No DB992525; one of the not-so-successful BR-designed equivalents of 1952-54 to Diagram 1/585 and running on plate-frame bogies. This is lettered 'Stone Only. Empty to Meldon Quarry Okehampton' but has recently been changed from another location. All four are branded 'Walrus' and some have bauxite patches upon which the lettering is superimposed, others are black overall. A Southern Diagram 1578 'pillbox' brings up the rear. *M Rhodes*

After the debacle of BR Diagram 1/585, further exacerbated when the 50-ton 'Whale' to Diagram 1/589 was introduced, a return was made in 1970 to the best 40-ton hopper design: the Southern Railway one of 1947! These were coded 'Sealion' and 'Seacow', and were a modernised version of SR Diagram 1775. BR Diagrams 1/590 and 591 respectively were allocated and a combined total in excess of 700 were built over the years from 1970 to 1982. 'Sealion' No DB982686 is seen when fairly new in olive green at Blackwater in 1976. This runs on French-designed cast-steel bogies. Note also the extended ballast chutes. By now no brake van is needed on the rear of the train – just a tail lamp. *M Rhodes*

The unique SECR ballast plough brake van formed the starting point for the Southern equivalent – indeed they were a direct copy of it and three more were built by Charles Roberts & Co in 1932. SR Diagram 1748 was allocated. Eight more were completed at Ashford in 1949 but with very minor detail differences – these became Diagram 1749. One of the latter – No DS62864 of April 1949 – is seen in 'Dutch' livery at Westenhanger in March 1992, showing evidence of much plate repair to the side and end planks. By now this has had its ploughs modified to enable it to be used as such over the third-rail – this had never been too successful before – and would not necessarily be so in the future either so it may come as no surprise to learn that withdrawal took place on 14 May 1996 – at Ipswich. It was then purchased by the Bluebell Railway, arriving there just 16 days later. Restoration has yet to commence. *M W F Gill*

Departmental Stock

8

While British Railways was predominantly a steam-hauled railway, it made sense to heat the carriages by the same means. However, as diesel and electric locomotives took over, or if steam heat was required long before the locomotive was coupled up, resort was made to a number of train heating boiler vans. The Southern Region rebuilt two Diagram 3141 special cattle vans (of the type described on pages 77-79) in November 1962. These were oil-fired and numbered DS70190/91 in the departmental series; they were formerly special cattle vans Nos 3716 and 3703 respectively. Departmental Diagram 1963 was allocated and this states that the oil tank capacity was 360 gallons while the water tank held 1,000 gallons. The vehicles tared 15 tons and this increased to 21½ tons in full working order. The underframes saw relatively little modification save for improved springing but the bodywork has been extensively rebuilt. At first painted green, they had no specific allocation recorded in the registers and have been noted at various locations, including Bournemouth West, Weymouth, Ringwood, Salisbury (as here with No DS70191 seen in 1968, painted rail blue) and later on the Western Region at Reading and Oxford. The date of withdrawal of DS70190 was around 1988 but DS70191 was condemned in March 1982 and scrapped at Wards of Briton Ferry in the following August. *M Rhodes*

Southern Rolling Stock in Colour

Eight – Departmental Stock

Opposite top: Five more train heating boilers were built between December 1962 and March 1963 – coinciding with one of the harshest winters of last century! These were rather different and were built on the underframes of former SR 21-ton mineral wagons. Numbered DS70185-89, these featured bodywork to the British Railways Mk 1 profile and presented a rather more modern appearance. Diagram 1964 was allocated and this informs us that the oil tank was again of 360 gallons capacity but the water tank held 1,100 gallons. The tare weight was 14 tons 4 cwt and the weight in working order was 21 tons. Dimensions were 21ft 6in long on a 12ft underframe. These were all allocated to Southampton Docks – where of course there was no main-line locomotive depot but much carriage stock could be awaiting departure for some time without a locomotive attached. Three may be seen in the picture, with No DS70185 nearest the camera. All are painted in Southern Region green livery. Nos DS70186/87/89 were later moved to Clapham Junction while No DS70185 went to Bristol, No DS70188 to Oxford. Those at Clapham were withdrawn between 1976 and 1980 and broken up at Swindon – dates of disposal of the others are not known. *NB collection*

Opposite bottom: A number of match wagons for Plasser ballast cleaners were converted from former utility van underframes during 1967, numbered DS70252-55. This is No DS70253, seen in olive green livery at Guildford in May 1970. The underframe was previously under Covcar No 2434, which dates originally from October 1931 and was withdrawn in April 1967, being rebuilt a month later into the form seen. The parentage of the underframe is obvious when compared with the originals on pages 72-75. The vehicle may still be in service today. *M Rhodes*

In the days when many coaches were lit by gas, tank wagons supplying this to outstations were a very common sight. The tanks themselves were very soundly constructed and it was usual procedure to mount them on old carriage or passenger van underframes – each tank often lasting for many years and being transferred from one underframe to another as the latter wore out. The Southern phased out carriage gas lighting around 1938 but other fixed locations at stations and workshops still needed mobile supplies so a smaller number of tanks remained in use. Latterly, many of these simply sat around awaiting withdrawal. This anonymous four-wheel example is seen at Eastleigh Works on 9 August 1961. Positive identification is not possible, but the underframe came from an ex-LSWR 24ft passenger luggage van of the type seen on page 16. In Southern days these tank wagons might be painted grey, red oxide or black, but in BR days rust was the more usual finish. After 1948 they were all renumbered into departmental series numbers between DS2001 and DS2133. The lower numbered examples were generally four- or six-wheel; some of the higher numbered tanks were bogie vehicles. *M Rhodes*

Southern Rolling Stock in Colour

This rather curious piece of equipment at Guildford yard in 1964 is tunnel inspection truck No DS658 – albeit appearing anonymous. This was constructed on the shortened underframe of a former LSWR coach: 56ft four-compartment corridor brake third No 3108, which had been transferred to departmental stock as mess coach No 1775s in November 1947. This was withdrawn in February 1953 and the underframe reused four months later as the basis of the inspection vehicle. The metal framework could be swung out over an adjacent track on either side and then used as a working platform, or as a staging point upon which further scaffolding could be erected to reach the underside of a high bridge or building for repointing and other maintenance work. When first converted, the vehicle had a timber hut-like structure at the right-hand end, but this was later removed. Departmental series Diagram 1940 was allocated and this gives the length as 37ft 7in over headstocks, while the framework was 19ft 6in long overall and 7ft 4in wide when retracted. The working platform was 13ft 9in wide when fully extended. This unusual vehicle was withdrawn in March 1974. *M Rhodes*

Eight – Departmental Stock

Former LSWR 3,500-gallon tender No 191, as converted to water tank No DS3001 in October 1949, seen at Salisbury in January 1967. The tender was built in 1902 and was attached to 'K10' class 4-4-0 No 146 from then until withdrawal in February 1948. The photographer notes that, by looking against the light, the letters LSWR, Maunsell style lettering Southern 146 and the word Southern in Bulleid style could be seen from some angles. In the picture, the last Bulleid lettering and the remnants of Maunsell green plus the lining may just be seen. The railway used these tenders to deliver water to remote and outlying locations – quite a number of which had no mains water supply. This was the first use of the DS3000 number series, which reached DS3346 and was used over the period 1949-55, although many numbers were allocated to Wickham permanent way trolleys and the like. This tender was finally withdrawn in November 1969. *M Rhodes*

The Southern purchased eight small hand cranes from Messrs Booth Brothers at various times between 1930 and 1943 for use by the Commercial Department. These could be ordered to any station to assist with the loading or unloading of a particularly heavy or awkward load, or be hired to other departments for construction work and the like. All were numbered in the departmental series. No DS1748 was one of three 12-tonners bought in October 1943 – along with two 6-ton machines – at a time when much wartime traffic was passing through a number of country stations that did not possess a static crane. Numbers were then 1746/47s for the lighter four-wheel cranes, 1748-50s for the heavier six-wheel version. In fact, No 1748s was specifically purchased on behalf of the Government and was not actually taken into Southern Region stock until January 1951, although in terms of usage this was probably academic. Five identical match trucks were completed at Ashford to run with them, these carrying the same number as their crane, but suffixed 'sm' (skillet match). They were completed in January 1943 – some months before the cranes arrived – the one to accompany the Ministry of War Transport crane being, significantly, the subject of a separate order. The former MWT crane is seen at Farnborough North in 1967, being used for the construction of a new electrical substation at a site where road access was difficult. The match truck has now been renumbered as DS3182; this took place as late as June 1960. The crane is now black with a white tip to the jib and red headstocks, although parts appear to be in red oxide primer, while the skillet has a grey superstructure with black underframe. This was to a standard RCH specification: 17ft 6in long with a wheelbase of 10ft. The crane was 21ft long over headstocks. Note that the match truck has a vacuum cylinder, while the crane itself is merely through piped. The pair were officially withdrawn in September 1972, although they were both purchased by, and arrived on, the Bluebell Railway three months earlier! Both have been restored to Southern Railway livery and are currently operational. *M Rhodes*

Eight – Departmental Stock

Altogether very much more impressive is steam-powered breakdown crane No DS81, seen at Stewarts Lane in August 1966. Built by Ransomes & Rapier in November 1927, it was of 36 tons capacity and went new to Brighton, moving to Fratton in August 1946, Feltham by 1958 and Stewarts Lane since 1963. Finally withdrawn in February 1986, it was then purchased by the Kent & East Sussex Railway. The bogie match truck was originally numbered 81sm, becoming DS3088 in November 1953. This was also built by Ransomes & Rapier. The livery is lined black, with some moving parts and the works plates picked out in red. For a picture of the opposite side see *Southern Wagons in Colour*, Plate 158. *R C Riley, courtesy Rodney Lissenden*

On 20 February 1960, 'Battle of Britain' pacific No 34084 *253 Squadron* set off with a freight to Bricklayers Arms from Hither Green yard against a red signal – running slowly through the stop blocks and down the embankment – coming to rest on its side adjacent to the yard approach road. Luckily there were no injuries – just shock and embarrassment for the crew. This was the scene on the following day as the recovery operation commenced – which proved difficult and protracted. Ransomes & Rapier 36-ton crane No DS1197 is in attendance but only the tender was recovered on that day. This crane was one of a pair (the other was No 1196s) built in December 1937 and was allocated to Bricklayers Arms. It carries the same livery as No DS81 in the previous picture but with the earlier 'cycling lion' emblem. Later the crane moved on to Hither Green and finally Brighton, by which time it was painted red. The two short four-wheel carrying trucks fore and aft are part of the crane and were all classed as DS1197. The four-wheel match truck beyond (originally numbered 1197sm) is now No DS3093, renumbered in May 1956, although one official record gives the date as November 1955. An 'N' class mogul provides the motive power for the crane. *R C Riley, courtesy Rodney Lissenden*

Eight – Departmental Stock

On 8 March 1965 there was a spectacular goods train derailment at Streatham Common, resulting in the destruction of quite a number of wagons, fortunately without injury to persons. Amongst the vehicles damaged were ex-SECR utility van No DS448 (the van in green livery and part-covered by a tarpaulin seen under the crane jib), another departmental SR utility van in gulf red, two Borails and some continental ferry vans – giving some idea of the diverse stock that might be seen in such a train at that time. Two cranes attended – a smart modern red one from Hither Green, seen in the background, and this rather scruffy Permanent Way steam crane. It appears to be a Taylor & Hubbard product – one of Nos DS56/57/58 built for the Civil Engineer in 1956 or Nos DS414/15/16 built in 1948. The most likely contenders are one of Nos DS56, DS57 or DS416, which were based at Purley, Beddington Lane and New Cross Gate during the 1950s and 1960s. The others were allocated to the South Western section at Woking, Eastleigh and the Exeter district and so are less likely to be seen on the Central section. Without a number or depot allocation being visible, further identification is not possible. All four running lines were blocked and clearance took some time; normal traffic not being resumed until 11 March. *M W F Gill*

Index

Accidents –
    Hither Green 133
    Streatham Common...............12, 133
Air control vans.................14, 37, 46, 47

Bluebell Railway.........16, 17, 24, 26, 27, 29, 36, 39, 49, 54, 75, 87, 124, 130
Blue Circle cement vans 110, 111
Bogies 19, 91, 92
Bournemouth Belle 60, 62, 63, 65
BP oil tank....................................110
Breakdown cranes............131, 132-133
Breakdown vans 7, 10-12, 23, 50, 73
BR Mk 1 stock –
    Corridors 57, 60
    Non-corridors............................58, 59
Bulleid stock –
    59ft multi door........................50, 51
    64ft 6in multi door..................50, 52
    Post 1945 corridors ....3, 43, 52-57, rear cover
    Livery.......................................42, 43, 56

Camping coaches –
    SR 8, 9
    Pullman......................................61-64
Chipman Weedkilling Company 51
Compass Rose rail tour (REC) 36
Covcar/CCT 75, 109
Cranes..................96, 100, 130-133
Crimson lake & cream livery........43, 44, 52, 53

Dean Forest Railway 120
Departmental stock –
    Boiler vans..............................125, 126
    Cranes 96, 100, 130-133
    Gas tank 127
    Match trucks 96, 100, 126, 127
    Numbering 127, 129
    Tunnel truck 128
    Water tank 129
Devon Belle 65, 67

Electric stock................................25, 43
Elephant vans 76
Express Dairies.................10, 81, 84, 85

Freshwater Yarmouth & Newport Rly 102
Fruit vans 5, 15, 75

G class Pullmans 64
GPO vans 28, 71, 76
GW Society, Didcot 82
Gas tanks 127
Golden Arrow 65, 68, 71
Goods Department cranes..96, 100, 130
Grounded vehicles –
    Coaches 5, 25, 30, 40
    Vans....................15, 25, 40, 101, 102

H class Pullmans 62, 63

Imperial Airways service.....................67
Isle of Wight Railway 100, 101
Isle of Wight Central Railway....100, 102
Isle of Wight Steam Railway 20, 21, 32, 96, 98, 101
Isle of Wight stock –
    Coaches 15, 20-22, 30-34
    Wagons........................88-91, 94-102
Internal user numbering...........6, 11, 44, 101, 108

K class Pullmans 60, 65-68
Kent & East Sussex Railway........8, 9, 19, 118, 131

Lancing Works train 26

LBSCR coaching stock –
    4-wheel 30
    6-wheel 40
    54ft bogie............................20, 31-34
    Pull-push 35-38
    Saloon 39
LBSCR wagon stock –
    Brake vans 102
    Cattle wagon 96
    Machinery truck..........................99
    Open goods 94-96
    Single bolsters.....................91, 97-99
LCDR stock.....................................29, 32
LMS GPO vans 76
LSWR coaching stock –
    6-wheel 5
    56ft non-corr 6-10
    Corridor 8, 9
    Ironclads 10-15, 43
    Pull-push 10, 14, 27
    Restaurant car................................15
    Saloons....................................10, 11
Luggage vans 15, 16, 25, 127
LSWR wagon stock –
    Bogie bolsters..........................90, 91
    Brake vans..........................88-91, 97
    Match trucks 96, 100
    Open goods...................................88
    Water tank 129
Longmoor Military Railway..........10, 11, 18, 19, 92, 118

Maunsell stock –
    Restriction 0..................................50
    Restriction 1 ....3, 39, 47-49
    Restriction 4......................41-45, 59
    Restaurant cars...................26, 41, 43
    Pull-push sets 46, 47, 58
Mid-Hants Railway 30

Index

Milk Tanks/Trucks ....Front cover, 2, 80-87
Milk Tank numbering/Diagrams 81
Ministry of War Transport 81, 85-87, 130
Peak Rail, Matlock 119
Plasser match wagon................126, 127
Plum & spilt milk livery 43, 52
PMV luggage vans 72-74
Private owner wagons –
    Cement vans 110, 111
    Minerals 108, 109
    Tank wagons............................88, 110
Pullmans –
    G class 64
    H class 62, 63
    K class 60, 65-68
    S class 61
    12-wheel......................................61-63

Saloon coaches 10, 11, 19, 39
S class Pullmans................................61
Scenery vans......................................76
Scrapping stock at Newhaven........6, 25, 37, 38

SECR coaching stock –
    Birdcage.........................17-19, 23-26
    GPO vans...28
    IOW rebuilds..............................20-22
    Long tens.................................10, 26, 27
    Luggage vans...............................22, 40
    Steel panelled 26
SECR wagon stock – Brake vans..........93
Shell/BP tank wagons 88, 110
SNCF mineral wagon 108
Southern Belle 61, 62
Southern coach liveries 41, 43
Southern wagons –
    Ballast brake................................124
    Ballast hoppers 122, 123
    Banana vans 115, 116
    Borail (bolster) 121
    Brake vans- 4 wheel ..16, 95, 116-118
    Brake vans – bogie 119, 120
    Conflat D 109
    Covered goods 111-115
    Lowmac................................121, 122
    Machinery truck...................121, 122
    Match trucks 126, 127, 130-132
    Open goods 103-107
Special cattle vans 77-79

St Ivel milk tank 83
Stove fitted vans................................69
Swanage Railway 5, 119

Train heating boiler vans 125, 126
Trio A sets (SECR) 17-21
Trio C sets (SECR)...........................23-26
Tunnel inspection truck 128

United Dairies.................2, 80-84, 86, 87
Utility vans............14, 37, 46, 47, 69-76, 109, 133
Utility vans –
    electrically heated....................71, 72

Van B 69
Van C................................47, 48, 70, 71
Van U 75

War Department –
    Brake vans....................................118
    Rectank 92
Water tank..129
Waterloo & City line stock 95
Weedkilling train (IOW) 89, 100
West Park Dairy 81, 84

Also available from Mike King at Crécy Publishing

Southern Wagons in Colour

The first colour album devoted to the subject by acknowledged expert Mike King consists of close-up photographs of individual wagons from the SECR, LBSCR and LSWR as well as their SR counterparts – all are of course depicted in BR days. Detailed and informative captions accompany the colour images and compliment Southern Vans and Coaches in Colour.

ISBN: 9781909328198
Binding: Paper back
Pages: 112
Price: £17.50

Southern Vans & Coaches in Colour

A thorough and fascinating account of LSWR, LBSCR, SECR, SR (Maunsell and Bulleid), Pullman, BR Mk1 and Gresley vehicles in SR Green. With 175 colour images and detailed captions of vans of all sorts and sizes, Mike King's comprehensive research brings the subject to life.

ISBN: 9781909328310
Binding: paper back
Pages: 124
Price: £17.50

Crécy Publishing Ltd
1a Ringway Trading Est
Shadowmoss Rd
Manchester
M22 5LH
Order hotline 0161 499 0024
www.crecy.co.uk